Houseplants

4452
© 1995 Coombe Books
This edition published in 1995 by Coombe Books
for Parragon Book Service Ltd, Unit13-17
Avonbridge Trading Estate, Atlantic Road,
Avonbridge, Bristol BS11 9QD
Printed in Hong Kong
ISBN 1-85813-844-2

Houseplants

Text by
DAVID SQUIRE
Photography by
NEIL SUTHERLAND

‖ •PARRAGON• ‖

Contents

Introduction

Selecting and buying, watering and feeding, potting, propagating and displaying houseplants are fundamental facets of growing plants indoors. Growing plants in small pots in rooms or conservatories is not easy. Outdoors the cycle of seasons influences growth, and plants are always in harmony with their surroundings.

Indoors, however, plants are expected to thrive and create eye-catching displays although often living in conditions alien to them. Frequently there is a range of plants in a room, all demanding different temperatures and amounts of light. And although plants can be selected to suit varying amounts of light in a room, they all have to survive in the same temperature.

This book reveals the skills needed to look after houseplants, including what to look for when buying them, ways to judge if water is needed, feeding, top-dressing and repotting.

Houseplant enthusiasts invariably want to increase their plants but often believe it is difficult. Here the techniques of propagating these plants is revealed in step-by-step pictures. Displaying houseplants in eye-catching and unusual ways is as important as growing them successfully. These range from displaying plants singly or in groups to planting them in indoor hanging-baskets, bottles and terrariums.

Houseplant Care

Houseplants like all living things need care and attention if they are to survive and thrive in their home. Every factor, from the right type of soil to the amount of light each plant requires needs to be carefully considered.

Choosing and buying plants for the home, greenhouse and conservatory requires as much care as when buying any other item. Buying a low-cost plant that dies during the following week becomes an expensive buy. Don't buy plants with roots coming out of the drainage hole, or with wilting leaves. This indicates too dry or too wet potting compost. Watch out for plants which have no labels, or are displayed in cold and draughty positions, as their buds may later drop off. Never buy plants that are infested with pests and diseases or have compost covered in green slime.

Avoid any plants with bare stems and few leaves, or plants which are growing in small pots but have large amounts of foliage. Conversely, don't buy small plants in large pots.

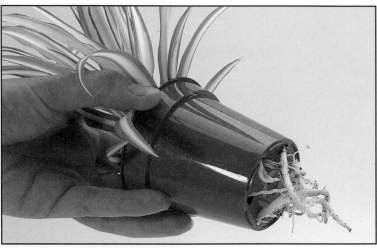

▲ Plants with roots coming out of drainage holes in their pots indicates that repotting is needed. If left for too long in this starved condition, plants seldom recover.

▶ Only buy flowering plants that have plenty of flower buds still to open. Plants bought while in full bloom only remain attractive for a limited period.

▲ Large plants in small pots are deprived of food.

▲ Small plants in large pots are difficult to water. When roots do not fill most of the pot, potting compost often becomes stagnant.

▲ Moss on pots indicates that the plant has remained too long in its pot and that growth may have been restricted. Although the moss can be removed, the plant may not recover.

▲ Healthy houseplants enrich a home for many months sometimes years. Damaged plants, as well as those infested with pests and diseases inevitably engender disappointment. The first step to success with houseplants is to inspect them carefully before buying, and then to get them home safely and quickly.

▲ Both clay and plastic pots – as well as loam-based and peat-based potting composts – grow healthy plants. Loam types are usually used in clay pots (left) and peat types in plastic pots (right).

▲ The pot should be in balance with the size of the plant, as shown here. Avoid large plants in small pots, and small plants in large pots, as it makes watering them very difficult.

Pots and potting compost are essential parts of growing plants indoors. Traditional pots for plants were made of clay, but during recent decades plastic ones have gained supremacy. However, both types enable plants to grow healthily, and both have advantages and disadvantages.

Range of sizes

Both clay and plastic pots are sold in a range of sizes, from 5cm (2in) to about 38cm (15in) wide. These measurements indicate the distance across the inside at the pot's top. The depth of a pot – whatever its size – is about the same as the width. Small pots increase in 12mm ($^1/_4$in) stages, larger ones in 2.5cm (1in) or 5cm (2in) increments.

Cache pots

Also known as cover pots, they cover growing pots, creating an attractive feature as well as complementing and highlighting home decor. Most are round, plain or decorated, and in a wide colour range. However, some – and especially larger types – are square, with the largest mounted on castors to enable easy movement.

The prime danger with cache pots is that when plants are watered, excess water may remain in their bases and eventually cause roots to decay. Therefore, about ten minutes after watering a plant, tip away water accumulated in the cache pot's base.

Saucers

Because growing pots have holes in their bases to allow excess water to drain, they must be stood in saucers – or placed in cache pots – to prevent water spoiling decorative surfaces.

They are available many colours and designs, some matching the growing pot to create a co-ordinated design.

Potting composts

Garden soil is not suitable for growing plants in pots indoors, as it is variable in quality, often badly drained and may contain weed seeds, pests and diseases. Specially-prepared potting composts are needed and basically there are two types – 'loam-based' and 'peat-based'. However, plants can be grown without any potting compost and this is known as hydroculture, also known as hydroponics.

Loam-based potting composts are formed from sterilized soil, sharp sand and peat, whereas peat-based types are wholly created from peat. Both have advantages and disadvantages.

Garden soil

Peat based compost

Loam based compost

◄ Houseplants in garden soil (left) under achieve and are quickly killed by soil pests and diseases. Both loam-based (centre) and peat-based potting composts (right) successfully grow houseplants.

Light and warmth – in nature provided by sunlight – are vital for healthy growth, activating the growing process in plants. In nature, light and warmth are in harmony and balance, the temperature rising with an increase in light intensity. There is also a close relationship between the seasons and light and warmth. Plants indoors, however, are often expected to thrive in high temperatures and low light.

▲ Strong light is just as harmful as too little. This peperomia has been exposed to strong light, causing leaves to wilt and shrivel. Thick-leaved plants are less affected than thin-leaved types.

▲ This peperomia has been given slight shade so is still healthy.

◄ Plants that are deprived of light become unsightly and eventually deteriorate to a point when recovery is impossible. This variegated plant has been kept in a dark position.

► This variegated plant however has been well looked after with good lighting and watering and it certainly shows.

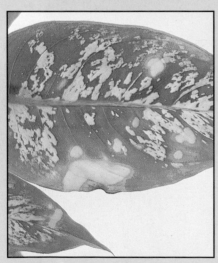

▲ Leaves form blisters when water droplets fall on them and are then exposed to strong sunlight. The water acts as a lens, intensifying the light and burning the leaf.

▲ Plants naturally grow towards light, their stems and leaves bending over in an unsightly manner. Therefore, every few days turn foliage plants a quarter of a turn.

▲ This plant has an even growth because it has been turned regularly.

▲ Rapidly changing temperatures between day and night – and especially within the period of light – soon cause leaves to fall off. Too wet or dry compost also contributes to the fall of leaves.

▲ Plants with thicker tougher leaves are not damaged so severely.

Houseplant enthusiasts who live in basements or dark-roomed houses can use 'growing lights' suspended over plants to supplement low light. This is especially useful in winter to keep plants healthy and growing. The light source is suspended 15-30cm (6-12in) above flowering plants, and 30-60cm (1-2ft) above those primarily grown for their attractive foliage.

Use the lights about twelve hours each day. Do not leave them on all night.

▲ High temperatures, low humidity and dry potting compost cause plants to wilt and the foliage to shrivel. Leaves become crisp and dry, eventually falling off and creating an unsightly plant.

▲ Plants that are placed in more conducive conditions retain their glossy leaves.

▲ Growing a plant in low temperatures is just as damaging as when too high. The plant ceases to grow, eventually collapsing – leaves and flowers around the outside are affected first.

Like all living things, plants are formed mainly of water, and without it they soon die. Plants absorb water through small, hair-like roots. The moisture moves into larger roots and then to stems and eventually leaves. From there it passes into the atmosphere through small pores known as stoma — mainly found on the undersides of the leaves. This is known as transpiration and as well as keeping the plant cool, firm and upright, it enables the absorption of plant foods from the potting compost and its subsequent movement within a plant. More houseplants die through being excessively or insufficiently watered than from any other reason.

1. Rubbing a finger or thumb on potting compost to assess its moisture content is the most popular method of judging if water is needed. However, repeated pressing tends to compress the compost.

2. The colour of potting compost indicates if water is needed. When dry, it becomes pale and crumbly, but if wet is dark. Most houseplant enthusiasts use this method.

Judging when a plant in a pot needs water is a skill derived from experience, although in recent years specialized equipment has become available to take the guess-work out of this task. If you are happy with your skills the specialist equipment may not be worthwhile.

3. Tapping a clay pot with a cotton-reel (bobbin) attached to a short stick indicates the degree of moisture: the pot rings if water is needed, but is dull when wet. This only works on clay pots.

4. Moisture-indicator strips – also known as watering signals – are relatively new. They are inserted into potting compost and the amount of moisture is indicated by the strip.

5. Moisture-meters are widely available and indicate when soil or compost needs water. They are very efficient and precise, but repeated insertions of the probe eventually damages roots.

P lants are individual in their need for water, some requiring more than others. Large plants need more water than small ones, while in winter and when dormant they need less water than in summer. Also, large plants in small pots need more frequent watering than when in large pots. There are two ways in which to water houseplants.

▲ Watering 'over the rim' is the usual way to apply water, filling the space between the potting compost and rim. Allow excess to filter through to a saucer, emptying it after half an hour.

▶ Soft and hairy leaves are damaged if water falls on them. Water these plants by standing the pot in a bowl of water until moisture reaches the surface. Then remove and allow excess to drain.

The amount of moisture in the air influences the health and growth of plants. Desert cacti live in arid and hot regions and have thick outer layers that reduce the amount of moisture they give off. Most plants, however, need a humid atmosphere if their leaves and stems are not to become dry.

The perceived humidity of air is closely related to the temperature.

The higher the temperature, the larger the amount of moisture it can hold. In winter, when the air is quite dry, rooms in which the temperature is high can, as far as plants are concerned, become like deserts.

This is not a problem for cacti, but jungle plants soon suffer — both flowering and foliage types if they are not given enough moisture.

▲ Placing plants in groups creates humid micro-climates around them. Moisture given off from the surfaces of leaves is trapped. When a plant is displayed on its own, moisture soon disperses.

Double potting

Some foliage houseplants can be given both a humid atmosphere and cool roots by potting them in two pots, one inside the other. A layer of moist peat between two pots protects the potting compost from excessive warmth, while the moist peat creates humidity around the leaves.

Only clay pots can be used for double-potting.

1. Select a clay pot about 5cm (2in) wider than the clay pot in which a plant is growing.

2. Place moist peat in its base and put the smaller one inside. The two rims must be level. Fill the space between them with moist peat. It is usually necessary to use a small stick to compress the peat. Ensure that the inner pot is in the centre of the outer one, and not lop-sided.

3. Use a small jug to moisten the peat between the pots. Allow excess water to drain, ensuring the peat is not totally saturated. Regularly check that the peat is moist, especially during summer.

When plants fill their pots with roots they must be repotted. To neglect this task results in a plant becoming stunted and not achieving its full size. It is essential that plants are progressively moved only in small stages from one pot to a larger one. If small plants are moved into too large pots, their roots are then surrounded by masses of potting compost and it is difficult to keep the moisture content at the right level. When potting compost in a pot is filled with roots, excess moisture is rapidly absorbed and given off by the plant through the leaves, preventing the potting compost becoming totally saturated and eventually unsuitable for plants.

▲ Many cacti have stiff and sharp spines and therefore need to be handled carefully. When repotting them either use gloves or hold the plant firm by encircling it with a band formed of folded newspapers.

1. Thoroughly water the plant a few days before repotting it – a dry soil-ball does not encourage rapid establishment. Tap the pot's rim on a firm surface while supporting the soil-ball.

2. Check that the roots are healthy and not infested by root pests, such as root mealy bugs. Select a clean pot that is slightly larger than the previous one.

3. Place some potting compost in the pot's base, so that the surface of the root-ball is about 12mm ($^1/_4$in) below the new pot's rim. Then, trickle potting compost around the root-ball.

4. Gently firm potting compost around the root-ball until it is 12mm ($^1/_4$in) below the rim. Later in the plant's life, when larger pots are used, leave a larger space at the top.

5. Water the potting compost 'over the rim', rather than by standing the pot in a bowl shallowly filled with water. Watering this way settles compost around the roots.

1. Before using a liquid fertilizer, carefully read the instructions. Never use more fertilizer than recommended.

2. Thoroughly agitate the water to ensure that the water is completely mixed.

3. Do not apply liquid fertilizers to dry compost as it may damage the roots.

Plants need a balanced diet of nutrients if they are to remain healthy and live for a long time. Most plants under-achieve, as they are usually starved. Regular feeding during a plant's growing period can make a remarkable difference. Both foliage and summer-flowering houseplants are normally fed from early spring to late summer (at 10-14 day intervals), while they are growing strongly. Winter-flowering plants, however, can be fed at about 14-day intervals during the period they remain in flower.

▲ Misting the leaves of some plants with a weak mixture of water and liquid fertilizer is good for plants with smooth leaves.

Plants need different amounts of food at certain times in their development; to create a strong root-system (phosphates), masses of leaves and stems (nitrogen), or a wealth of flowers (potash). Houseplants are usually bought when young and perhaps still using the nutrients in the potting compost into which they were initially potted. Once they have completely used this food supply they need regular feeding.

▲ Push feeding sticks into the compost just in from the pot's side. This is where most of the feeding roots are situated.

▲ Pills can also be inserted into the compost.

1. When plants in pots become too large to be repotted, they are topdressed in spring. Allow the surface soil to dry slightly, then use a small trowel to scrape away the top 2.5-3.6cm (1-2$\frac{1}{2}$in). Use a small fork to prick over the surface, taking care not to damage the plant's roots. If it is evident that there are masses of surface roots, neglect this forking job.

2. Replace the surface scrapings with fresh potting compost. Leave a space between the top of the compost and the rim, so that the plant can be watered when the potting compost becomes dry.

Air plants

1. Many bromeliads have urns at their centres, through which they are watered and fed. Once a month from spring to late summer, pour a weak solution (about a quarter of the normal strength) of a liquid fertilizer into the urn.

2. Air-plants (Tillandsias) are adapted to live in humid places. Feed by misting the leaves with a weak solution (about a quarter of the normal strength solution) of a liquid fertilizer once a month from spring to late summer.

Grooming plants so they look their best is an essential part of growing houseplants. By the removal of dead flowers the flowering period can be extended. Also, the removal of shoot tips encourages a neat and attractive plant, while supporting and training stems creates a neat appearance.

1. Carefully curl and train shoots around the support, taking care not to bend or kink them. Repeat this task several times throughout summer, and regularly feed the plant to encourage growth.

2. From early autumn to late spring, Jasminum polyanthum creates a wealth of pink or pale-pink flowers, usually trained around a large hoop of pliable canes, or a white or green plastic loop.

3. When young plants have shoots 25-45cm (10-18in) long, insert the support into the potting compost. Pliable canes are just pushed into it, while plastic loops are attached to the rim.

Some plants have a sprawling, scrambling and climbing nature and although this is often part of their attraction occasionally stems need to be trimmed. Always trim them back to a leaf-joint, using a sharp knife, secateurs, scissors or just by holding the stem firmly and snapping it sideways. Never leave a short piece of stem, as this encourages the onset of decay.

1. Slightly woody stems, such as those on azaleas, are best trimmed with sharp scissors, cutting back to a leaf-joint. This encourages bushiness and the development of sideshoots.

2. Encourage young plants to form a bushy base by nipping back young shoots to leaf-joints. If this job is neglected, plants become bare at their bases and their appearances are spoilt.

Flowering houseplants, as well as those in greenhouses and conservatories, need regular checking when in flower. Decaying flowers left on plants encourage others to rot, and the decay may then spread to soft leaves. Also, the removal of dead flowers encourages the development of others.

Pinch off dead flowers from azaleas. Do not leave parts of flowers, as this encourages the onset of decay around soft shoots. Hold the shoot firmly while carrying out this task.

Dust and dirt are the enemies of leaves, spoiling their appearance, clogging pores and preventing the sun reaching them. Proprietary, ozone-friendly sprays are available, and these are ideal for large-leaved plants, while hairy-leaved types and bristly cacti can be cleaned with small soft brush.

1. Support large leaves with one hand and gently wipe with a damp cloth or spray with a leaf-cleaner. Do not do this when the plant is in strong light, as the sun's rays may cause damage.

2. Clean plants with many small leaves by gently swirling them in a bowl of clean water, allowing excess to drain and dry in gentle warmth but away from direct and strong sunlight.

3. Remove dirt and dust from bristly cacti, as well as hairy-leaved plants, by using a small soft brush. Blowing strongly on leaves while brushing also helps in the removal of dirt.

1. Remove all faded flowers, as well as those which will be past their best by the time you expect to return. If left, they decay and encourage the rest of the plant to deteriorate.

Carefully looking after houseplants throughout the year and then for them to die through neglect while you are holidaying away from home is a major disaster. Your plants main need while you are away on holiday is water, and although a neighbour will often act as a 'plant sitter' unless that person is experienced in looking after plants it is usually better to rig up your own watering system. Houseplant sitters who are not used to looking after indoor plants invariably

2. Remove dead leaves from foliage plants. Those with masses of foliage are soon damaged by decaying leaves that are left in position, the rot quickly spreading.

3. Place small plants on a capillary mat, one end spread over a draining-board and the other trailing into a sink full of water, which acts as a large reservoir – ideal for long holidays.

4. Use wicks to water plants individually. Push one end of a wick into the potting compost, the other deeply into a reservoir of water positioned slightly higher than the plants.

excessively water them, with the result that roots rot and eventually the plants die – sometimes weeks after you return from holiday.

The length of the holiday, as well as whether in winter or summer, influences the treatment given to the plants.

Prevention is much easier than trying to eliminate an established colony of pests or a severe infection from disease. It is far better to take a few preventative measures like buying plants only from reliable and reputable sources, inspecting new plants as soon as you get them home and checking plants regularly – perhaps when watering them – to ensure they are clean.

Types of pests
Aphids
Also known as greenfly, blackfly, aphis and aphides, these insect are the main pest of plants. They are small, soft-bodied, sap-sucking insects, usually green but may be grey, orange or black. In homes, greenhouses and conservatories the green form is normally seen. Aphids damage soft parts such as petals, shoot tips and young leaves are attacked, aphids piercing the tissue, sucking sap and causing mottling and distortion. Spray plants as soon

as these pests are seen, using insecticides containing dimethoate, malathion, pirimiphos-methyl with pyrethrins, or resmethrin and pyrethrum.

Cyclamen mites
These pernicious pests attack a wide range of houseplants, including cyclamen, pelargoniums, African Violets and Busy Lizzies. The mites are minute, eight-legged, spider-like creatures which cluster on the undersides of leaves and look like a coating of dust. Young mites are almost transparent; adult females vary from milky white to brown. You can see the damage on the outside of the leaves which become wrinkled into depressions and pockets. Infested foliage becomes darker than normal and the flowering period is shortened.

Red spider mites
Also known as greenhouse red spider mites and glasshouse red spider mites, they attack carnations, chrysanthemums and other ornamental plants, as well as tomatoes and cucumbers in greenhouses. These mites are about the size of a pin-head, and vary in colour from a transparent yellow-white through green to orange and brick-red. In winter the colour tends to be red, whereas in summer when females are breeding they are lighter in colour. Both adult and immature mites pierce and suck the undersides of leaves, causing a fine, light mottling on upper surfaces which, if the attack is severe, become yellow and blotched. They often create webs. Daily mist-spraying plants prevents an attack developing into epidemic proportions – but do not syringe flowers or soft and hairy leaves.

Mealy bugs

Mainly sub-tropical and tropical pests. Plants attacked include palms, ferns, vines, azaleas and hippeastrums. The bugs are white, waxy, woodlice-like creatures that live in groups. If ignored they form large colonies. They suck sap, causing distortion, loss of vigour and yellowing of the leaves. Like aphids they excrete honeydew, encouraging the presence of sooty mould. They form colonies in leaf-joints, along stems and on leaves. The best treatment is to wipe off infestations with cotton-buds or cotton-swabs dipped in methylated spirits – sometimes known as rubbing alcohol. Spray established colonies with malathion. Burn seriously infested plants.

Root mealy bugs

These are closely related to mealy bugs, but instead of attacking leaves, stems and shoots, they infest roots. They mainly live on the outer roots of plants in pots, especially infesting cacti and other succulents. The bugs look like waxy-woodlice. They upset the normal root functions, resulting in foliage discoloration and wilting plants. If untreated, the plant will die. To stop use a solution of malathion to drench the roots and soil-ball.

Scale insects

The range of scale insects is wide, and plants attacked include fruit bushes and trees, ornamental trees, conifers, shrubs and roses, as well as orchids, ferns and other ornamental houseplants, indoors as well as in greenhouses, sunrooms and conservatories. Sign of attack is when plants become sticky. Swollen, protective, waxy-brown discs can be seen, and it is under these that female scale insects produce their young. Severe infestations cause speckling and yellowing of the leaves. Eradicating established colonies is difficult and plants are best burned.

Whitefly

Especially a nuisance in greenhouses, sunrooms and conservatories, infesting a wide range of plants. Tomatoes and cucumbers in greenhouses are often attacked. Whitefly is a moth-like insect with wings and a white, mealy covering. When disturbed, they flutter about the host plant. Mostly found on the undersides of leaves. Eradication is not easy, and several sprayings at 3-5 day intervals are necessary. Spray with malathion or pyrethrum.

Thrips

Several types infest plants in conservatories, sunrooms and greenhouses, although they are not major pests indoors. Thrips are tiny, dark brown, fly-like creatures, with light coloured wings and legs, often seen jumping or flying from plant to plant. Undersides of leaves develop small globules of a red liquid that eventually turns black, creating an unsightly mess. To kill thripes spray the plant with malathion or derris, repeating it several times.

Vine weevils

Serious pest in both its beetle-like adult form and when young as a larvae. Adult weevils are similar to beetles, but have a short snout. Each weevil is black and covered with short hairs that create a matt, dull appearance. Larvae are fat, legless and creamy-white; the head is brown with mouth parts adapted for chewing roots. Immediately the larvae or adults are seen, water the compost with malathion or a soil-pest killer. Also, spray the leaves.

Greenfly are one of the most common pests.

Earwigs

Few people have not seen an earwig. They attack outdoor plants as well as those in greenhouses, sunrooms and conservatories. Spray with malathion, although its often easier to pick them off. Shaking flowers and leaves in the morning soon dislodges them.

Sooty mould

Black, soot-like mould that lives on honeydew excreted by aphids and other sap-sucking insects. At first, the black, sooty deposit appears in clusters, but soon spreads and merges until the whole surface is covered. Wipe away light infestations with a damp cloth, and spray plant for aphids.

Rusts

Complicated diseases, seldom infesting plants indoors but frequently seen on carnations and chrysanthemums in conservatories, sunrooms and greenhouses. Remove and burn infected leaves. Increase ventilation – high humidity in sunrooms, conservatories and greenhouses encourages rusts.

Viruses

Microscopic particles that invade plants and animals, causing disorder in the tissue but seldom killing their host. Only the results can be seen, varying from deformed growth, mottled and streaked leaves to colour changes in flowers. There is no treatment for virus-infected plants. Remove and burn.

Botrytis

Also known as grey mould, this fungal disease is widespread and likely to occur on many plants. Spores are present in the air and if they land on wounds or decaying tissue, enter plants. To distroy cut off infected leaves. Remove dead flowers – if left they encourage the presence of botrytis. Damp, still air, as well as excessive watering, also encourages it. Spray infected plants with a fungicide.

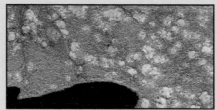

Rust on a chrysathemum leaf

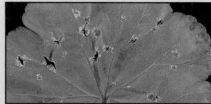

Pelargonium leaf curl virus

Black leg on a young pelargonium

Powdery mildew on a begonia

Botrytis on a cyclamen

Black leg

A disease mainly of cuttings – especially pelargoniums. Bases of stems become soft and black. Remove and destroy seriously infected cuttings. Slightly infected tissue can be cut away from valuable cuttings. Re-insert in clean potting soil. Ensure a good circulation of air over the cuttings and keep the potting compost barely moist.

Damping off

Attacks seedlings soon after germination. May also attack established plants in greenhouses, sunrooms and conservatories.

Powdery mildew

Fungal disease producing a white, powdery coating over leaves – often on both sides. Infects leaves, flowers and stems. Remove badly infected leaves, stems and flowers. Increase ventilation and keep the atmosphere drier.

Botrytis grey mould

paper. Too much water encourages the onset of decay, leaves becoming soft rather than brittle. Other causes of wilting: During very warm summer days – usually in late afternoons – houseplants with large amounts of foliage and growing in small pots may wilt slightly even though the compost is moist. This is because the plant is unable to absorb sufficient moisture to replace that lost by evaporation through the leaves. If the plant recovers by late evening or early morning, do not worry about the wilting. Some soil pests, such as root mealy bugs, graze on roots and make plants wilt. Remove the pot and check the soil-ball.

Flower buds fall off

This may happen if plants are in a draught, a dry atmosphere, receive a sudden chill or are knocked. Should a plant be affected, pick up the flower buds and place in a rubbish bin. If left they encourage the presence of diseases.

Leaves fall off

Occasionally, leaves fall off. If this happens quickly, it is probably due to the plant receiving a shock such as a sudden drop in temperature or

A s well as being harmed by pests and diseases, plants also become damaged and unhealthy because they are not grown properly.

Wilting

Growing houseplants in pots throughout the year and maintaining the right degree of moisture in the potting compost is not easy. Occasionally, plants wilt through being given either too much or too little water.

A houseplant's need for water varies throughout the year. Also, the size of the plant, the size of the pot and the amount of potting compost it holds influences the frequency and amount of water needed to maintain healthy growth.
Too little water: This is the main cause of wilting. Leaves and flowers wilt, eventually reaching a point when no matter how much water is given the plant will not recover. Leaves become crisp and brittle. This is just as likely to cause wilting as too little moisture, especially in winter when plants

may not be fully active and an excess of water is not quickly used. If plants are not badly affected, withhold the water until the potting compost becomes dry. Totally saturated compost can be encouraged to release moisture by removing the pot and either allowing air to circulate around the root-ball or wrapping it in absorbent

being placed in a cold draught. Reposition the plant in an even, warm temperature away from draughts. If leaves become yellow and slowly fall off, this is due to the plant being given too much water and the potting compost becoming waterlogged. Keeping plants in dark positions – and especially when combined with a lack of plant food such as nitrogen – also cause leaves to become yellow. Remove fallen leaves and do not give the plant further water until the root-ball has become moderately dry.

Green shoots

If green shoots appear on variegated plants, it is usually because the plant is in too dark a condition. The remedy is to move the plant into a brighter position. Occasionally, green shoots appear on a variegated plant, even when in good light. This is known as reversion and the offending shoots must be cut out at their bases.

Damaged leaf surfaces

If leaves become crisp and brown, this is due to insufficient water. But if white or straw-coloured patches or spots appear this is usually because water has splashed on leaves while the plant is in strong sunlight, the moisture then acting as a lens and intensifying sunlight. However, damage can also occur solely through plants that are best in slight shade being placed in direct sunlight.

Growing Houseplants

There are many ways to increase your stock of houseplants ranging from planting seed, taking cuttings and dividing by roots. This chapter also includes clever ideas for planting bulbs and displaying your plants.

Many houseplants can be increased from seeds, whether grown for their flowers, foliage or berries. Whatever the type of plant, the seeds need three basic conditions to encourage germination – moisture, warmth and air. These conditions are created by sowing seeds in a seed compost that both retains moisture yet allows air penetration, and either placing in a greenhouse or on a warm windowsill indoors.

2. Place more seed compost in the seed-tray and strike the surface level with a straight-edged piece of wood. When sowing seeds in seed-pans, use the top of a round jar as a firmer.

3. Using a piece of wood with a small handle attached to it, firm the surface until it is about 12mm ($^1/4$ in) below the rim. Keep the surface of the presser clean to ensure an even surface.

4. Tip the seeds into a folded, V-shaped piece of paper and gently tap the end to encourage them to fall on the compost. Do not sow seeds within 12mm ($^1/4$ in) of the edge. Label the box.

5. Some seeds require light to encourage germination, but most need darkness and are covered to three or four times their thickness. Use a finely-mesh sieve to scatter the compost.

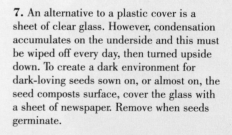

6. Water the seed compost by standing the seed-tray in a bowl of clean water. When moisture seeps to the surface, remove and allow to drain. Do not water from overhead, as this scatters the seeds. The seed-tray needs to be covered to prevent the surface of the seed compost drying, as well as maintaining a high temperature. Domed, plastic covers are convenient covers.

7. An alternative to a plastic cover is a sheet of clear glass. However, condensation accumulates on the underside and this must be wiped off every day, then turned upside down. To create a dark environment for dark-loving seeds sown on, or almost on, the seed composts surface, cover the glass with a sheet of newspaper. Remove when seeds germinate.

1. Fill a clean plastic seed-tray with seed compost. If small numbers of seeds are to be sown, use a shallow seed pan. Do not sow different seeds in the same containers. Using your fingers, firm the seed compost, especially around the sides and edges as this is where it will start to become dry if regular watering is neglected.

As soon as the seedlings are large enough to handle they must be moved to where they have more space and an increased amount of air and light. If not transferred (pricked out), they become drawn up, thin and lanky, and eventually unable to support themselves unless supported by neighbouring seedlings. Additionally, seedlings tightly clustered together are more susceptible to diseases than those with a good circulation of air around them.

1. After seeds germinate, remove the covering and allow air to circulate around the seedlings. Continue to water them by standing the seed-tray in a bowl of water. Avoid wetting the leaves. As soon as the seedlings are large enough to handle, transfer them individually into a potting compost in seed-trays. First, water the seed compost, then loosen a cluster with a small fork.

2. Place the seedlings on damp newspaper. Use a small dibber to make holes, keeping the outer row 12mm ($^1/_4$ in) from the edge, as this is where the potting compost first dries if watering is neglected.

3. Hold each seedling by a leaf, not its stem. Position each seedling at about the same depth as before, then gently lever potting compost against the roots, but taking care not to crush them. When the box is full of seedlings, gently tap the edges to level the loose surface. Water the seedlings from above to settle potting compost around their roots. Allow excess water to drain.

4. After the seedlings are established. The temperature should be slightly lowered and it is best to water the plants from below to prevent leaves becoming wet and also to help prevent the onset of diseases. Fresh air is vital for strong growth.

5. When the young plants are sturdy and growing strongly, transfer them into small pots of potting compost. First water, allowing excess to drain, then pot up individually. Avoid damaging roots. Fill a pot's base with potting compost, so that when potted the plant will be slightly lower than before. This allows for subsequent settlement of compost when watered. Then carefully fill in with potting compost.

ividing plants is perhaps the easiest way to increase plants. Eventually, many houseplants become congested, the pot packed with stems and roots. Many plants that grow very large can be repotted into larger pots, but some are better removed from their pots, divided into small pieces and repotted. Houseplants mainly grown for their attractive foliage are best divided in spring. Some flowering types with a perennial nature are also increased in this way, as soon as their flowers fade but preferably in spring. Flowering plants that finish flowering in autumn are best divided in spring. Division in spring enables young plants to become established during summer, while growing strongly. Congested houseplants usually have developed from one plant, originally central in the pot. Therefore, when dividing plants inspect the centres and if old discard them.

1. This congested Peace Lily (Spathiphyllum wallisii) is best divided in spring. Remove the soil-ball from the pot by inverting the plant and tapping the rim on a firm surface.

2. Evidence that division is needed is indicated by a mat of roots around the root-ball. A mass of white roots indicates that the plant is healthy and growing strongly.

3. Using fingers, tease and pull apart the root-ball into several substantially-sized pieces. It may be necessary to cut some roots, but never use a knife to slice through a plant.

4. Hold a plant in the centre of a pot and trickle fresh compost around the roots. Firm the potting compost.

5. Water the plants from above and place in a situation which will offer gentle warmth. It may be necessary to shade plants from strong sunlight until roots have become more established and are absorbing water.

Layering is an easy though not rapid way to increase many climbing and trailing houseplants with flexible stems. Long stems are secured with small pieces of wire into pots of potting compost. When roots form at the position where the shoot is pegged into the soil, it is severed from the parent plant. Late spring and early summer are the best times to layer plants, while they are growing strongly.

1. Below left: Water the mother plant to ensure the stems are turgid and not wilting. Prepare a pot by filling it with equal parts moist peat and sharp sand, firming it to within 12mm ($^1/_4$ in) of the rim.

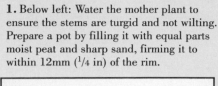

2. Bend the stem near to a leaf-joint and 10-15cm (4-6in) from its tip. This constricts – but does not sever – the stem, so that the flow of sap is restricted. Roots will form at this point.

3. Use a small piece of U-shaped wire to pin the shoot in the potting compost. Firm it around the bend, then water from above. Place both the mother plant and the layer in a plastic tray.

4. When rooted, young roots can be seen growing from the bend, together with fresh shoots from the shoot's tip. Use a knife to sever the layer from the mother plant.

Encouraging runners and plantlets to form roots is an interesting and easy method to increase plants. A few houseplants, such as the ever popular Spider Plant (Chlorophytum comosum) develops trailing stems with their new plantlets at the tips of these stems. The plantlets can be easily pegged into potting compost and they will then develop roots. A few plants have small plantlets along the surfaces of their leaves – or at their ends – that can be removed and encouraged to form roots in a similar way. The Chandelier Plant is a good example of this.

1. The Chandelier Plant (Kalanchoe tubiflora, but earlier known as Bryophyllum tubiflorum), develops clusters of small plantlets at the ends of its tubular leaves.

2. With age, the plantlets become large and develop hair-like roots that help to secure them in the potting compost. In nature, they fall and soon establishing themselves on damp soil.

3. Gently pull off several plantlets, taking care not to damage leaves. So that the mother plant retains an attractive appearance, remove plantlets from all over it, not just from one place.

4. Scatter plantlets on the surface of damp potting compost. They invariably fall in clusters and therefore need to be spaced by manipulating them with the tip of a knife.

5. Gently press plantlets into the potting compost. Water by standing the pot in a tray of water until moisture seeps to the top, then allow to drain. Place in gentle warmth on a shaded windowsill.

6. Keep moist and when the plantlets are rooted and have developed shoots, gently transplant into larger pots, either singly or three to a 7.5cm (3in) wide pot.

7. When established, place in a light place like a windowsill, and water well.

1. The Mexican Hat develops plantlets around the edges of its thick succulent leaves.

2. Gently pull off large and mature plantlets taking care not to remove thme from just one leaf.

3. Place the plantlcts on the surface of potting compost in a 7.5cm (3in) wide pot.

4. When rooted pot up young plants individually.

1. The spider plant develops long trailing stems with small plantlets at their ends. Use small pieces of bent wire to secure these plantlets into potting compost.

2. When the young shoots start to develop from the plantlets, sever the shoots from the parent plant.

Many houseplants can be increased from stem-tip cuttings, each formed from a piece of stem, several leaves and a terminal shoot. They are usually 7.5-13cm (3-5in) long and, if possible, taken from the outer area of the parent plant, where they would have been in good light and growing strongly. Spindly shoots are not suitable. Additionally, ensure that the mother plant is turgid – wilting plants never produce good cuttings. Cuttings need a moisture-retentive yet well aerated potting compost to encourage rooting, such as equal parts moist peat and sharp sand.

1. Use a sharp knife to cut a strong and healthy shoot from a mother plant, severing it just above a leaf-joint.

2. Do not leave short spurs, as they are unsightly and encourage the onset of decay. Trim the cutting's base to just below a leaf-joint, at the same time cutting off lower leaves close to the stem. Some cuttings have two leaves at each leaf-joint, others just one.

3. Dip the cutting's base in hormone rooting-powder. Use a small dibber to form a hole into which the stem is inserted 18-25mm ($^3/_4$-1in). Do not bury the lower leaves, as this encourages rotting.

4. Firm compost around the cutting's base, water from above, insert short split-canes in the potting compost and cover with a plastic bag. Secure its base around the pot with an elastic-band.

▼ Some plants grown in greenhouses have a slightly woody nature. these include the rose of China and Marginatus (here). In these cases the young shoots should be gently pulled from the stem so a small piece of woody stem is attached to the base.

S tem cuttings resemble stem-tip cuttings, but without a tip. It's an excellent way to increase plants with long, trailing stems. Additionally, it enables several cuttings to be created from a shoot, rather than just one as with stem-tip cuttings. Spring and early summer are the best times to take and root these cuttings, but if you have a propagation frame with soil-warming cables it is possible to take them throughout the year. However, by taking them in spring it ensures that cuttings are rooted and young plants established by the onset of winter. Ivies – especially the small-leaved types – are increased in this way.

1. Cut a long, young shoot from a parent plant. Do not use old and tough shoots. It is better to cut off an entire shoot, rather than to leave short, unsightly spurs on the mother plant.

2. Use a sharp knife to cut the shoot into several cuttings – ragged cuts do not heal quickly and produce roots. Cut slightly above each leaf-joint, leaving a piece of stem 36mm (1^1/2in) long.

3. Use a small dibber (or pencil) to insert cuttings 18-25mm (^{3}/4-1in) into equal parts moist peat and sharp sand. Firm each cutting – do not insert closer than 18mm (^{3}/4in) to the pot's edge.

4. Gently water the potting compost to settle it around the cuttings, and insert four short split-canes into the compost. Place a plastic bag over the canes and hold it firm with a rubber-band.

5. Place in gentle warmth and light shade. When young shoots develop from the leaf-joints, check that roots have formed. Remove the plastic bag and allow the cuttings plenty of fresh air.

▲ The new plant

6. Pot up rooted cuttings into pots of potting compost. Put either one, three or five cuttings in each pot – the higher the number of cuttings in a pot, the quicker a bushy plant is created.

Leaf-petiole cuttings are another good way of increasing your stock of plants. Each cutting is formed of a leaf together with the short stem (petiole) which would have attached it to the plant. The most popular plant raised in this way is Saintpaulia ionantha (African Violets)

1. In spring and early summer select a healthy plant. Use a sharp knife to cut off leaves with their leaf-stalks intact – avoid leaving short stumps. Take care not to spoil the plant's shape.

2. Use a sharp knife to trim back the stems to about 36mm(1¹/₂in) long. Stems are easily bruised and damaged, so take great care when handling and cutting them. Hold each cutting by its leaf.

3. Dip the end of each stem into a hormone rooting powder.

4. Place the dipped end into a pot full of compost. This rooting powder is often combined with a fungicide that helps to prevent diseases attacking the cuttings before they develop roots.

5. Firm the compost around the stems. Place two or three leaves in each pot. When small shoots appear, pot up into potting compost.

1. Instead of using compost African Violets can be rooted in water. Fill a glass bottle leaving 1.8cm (³/₄in) at the top.

2. Wrap a piece of paper over the top and secure with an elastic band. Gently pierce the paper with a sharp pointed knife.

3. Push the leaf stem through the hole so that its end just touches the water.

4. When the roots have developed pot up the leaf in potting compost.

Leaves of some houseplants, such as large-leaved begonias, can be encouraged to form roots along their undersides, with shoots developing from the upper surfaces. When established, these are separated and potted into small pots of potting compost.

1. Select a healthy leaf – free from pests and diseases – and sever the stem close to the plant's base. Do not leave a short piece of stem at the base, as it encourages the onset of diseases.

2. Turn the leaf upside down and with a sharp knife, sever the stem close to the leaf. Do not use old leaves that are stiff and brittle. Roots form more rapidly on young leaves.

3. Use a sharp knife or razor blade to cut across the veins on the underside of a leaf, about 18mm ($^3/_4$in) apart. Sever both the main and secondary veins.

4. Place the leaf vein-side downwards and press firmly so that it is in close contact with the potting compost in a plastic seed-tray. Hold the leaf in position with a few small stones.

5. An alternative way to keep the leaf in contact with the potting compost is to use small U-shaped pieces of wire. Insert them so that they are astride the main and secondary veins.

6. Place the plastic container in a bowl shallowly filled with water until moisture appears on the surface of the potting compost. Remove, allow to drain and cover with a transparent lid. Place in gentle warmth. Keep the potting compost moist and occasionally wipe condensation from the inside of the lid. Young plants eventually grow from the cut surfaces. Remove the lid.

7. When established, the young plants are transferred to small pots of potting compost. Don't constrict the roots and ensure each plant's base is not buried, as it encourages decay.

arge-leaved begonias can be increased by cutting their leaves into triangles and inserting them in compost. Young and healthy leaves root faster than old ones, and discard those that are damaged or infected by pests or diseases. A variation on leaf-triangles is leaf-squares. The triangles tend to be longer than the squares and therefore can be inserted deeper into the potting compost and given a firmer base. However, more leaf-squares, can be cut from a similarly-sized leaf.

1. Select a healthy leaf and sever it close to the plant's base. Avoid leaving short spurs. If only a few leaves are needed, cut from opposite sides to avoid spoiling the plant's shape. Turn the leaf upside down and cut off the stem, close to its base. Do not take leaves from plants growing in dry compost as they shrivel and do not produce roots.

2. Place the leaf on a flat piece of wood and cut it into triangles. The tip of the triangle should be towards the centre of the leaf. Several cuttings can be taken from one leaf.

3. Insert the cuttings, pointed-end downwards and to about half their length, in potting compost. Lightly water the cuttings from above, using a watering-can with a fine spray.

4. Cover with a translucent plastic lid, occasionally removing it to wipe away condensation. Periodically, check the potting compost is moist — water by standing the tray in water.

5. When rooted, carefully lever up plants and pot up individually into small pots of potting compost. Water the compost and place in gentle warmth until established and growing strongly.

As well as being increased from seeds, cacti and other succulents are frequently propagated from cuttings. Take cacti cuttings during spring and summer, from plants that are healthy and well watered. However, cuttings taken early in the year root faster than those in late summer, and will be well established by the onset of winter. Kitchen-gloves enable excessively spiny types to be handled with comfort.

1. Use a sharp knife to sever stems. Do not take too many cuttings from one plant – its shape will be spoilt. Young stems from around the outside of a clump root quicker than central old ones.

2. Do not immediately insert the cuttings into a rooting compost. Instead, allow their cut surfaces to dry for a few days. This enables them to root faster than if directly inserted.

3. Use equal parts moist peat and sharp sand. Sprinkle a thin layer of sand on the surface and then use a small dibber to create a hole into which the cutting can be inserted and firmed.

4. Lightly water the potting compost to settle it around each cutting and then place in gentle warmth. In spring and early summer rooting takes a few weeks, but later in the year is much longer.

Succulents such as some crassulas and echeverias can be increased from whole-leaf cuttings inserted upright in a sandy potting compost. Like most other cuttings, spring and early summer are the best times to take them. The succulent increased here is the Jade Plant (Crassula argentea).

1. Select a healthy, well watered plant and gently pull off mature and fleshy leaves close to the stem. Avoid leaving short spurs, as these will spoil the mother plant's shape.

2. Allow the cut surfaces to dry for a couple of days before inserting them in well drained and aerated potting compost, formed of equal parts moist peat and grit – with a surface layer of sharp sand.

3. Use a small dibber or knife to form a hole in the potting compost. Insert several cuttings in one pot, ensuring they are not close to the edges – this is where the potting compost first becomes dry.

4. Firm potting compost around the base of each leaf. Then lightly water and place in gentle warmth, but out of direct sunlight. Place in a propagation frame, or on a shaded window-sill.

5. When young shoots develop from the bases of the leaves, gently pot up into a sandy potting compost. Water and place in gently warmth until the young plants are established.

Yuccas, as well as dracaenas which have lost their lower leaves and have stiff, woody stems, can be increased by inserting cuttings vertically into potting compost.

These are frequently known as Ti-log cuttings, although often it is Dracaena terminalis — correctly known as Cordyline fruticosa and widely sold as C. terminalis — that is widely called the Ti Plant. It is also known as the Lucky Plant and Good Luck Plant. There is often confusion between dracaenas and cordylines: in general, the roots of dracaenas when cut are orange, while those of cordylines are white.

Ti-log cuttings can be bought from garden centres. Frequently, however, they are bought during holidays abroad. Cuttings from Brazil are sold as Lucky Plants and usually have their ends sealed with paraffin wax to reduce the rate at which they become dry. The top of each cane is indicated by a different coloured wax from that used at the base. This is to ensure that when potted the cane is not inserted the wrong way up — the instructions on the packaging indicates the colour coding.

1. Cut or scrape away wax from the lower end, but leave the wax on the top-end intact. This wax helps to prevent the loss of moisture from the cutting before it forms roots.

2. The cutting is inserted with the bare end downwards into the compost, the top still covered with wax. Do not use a very large pot, as this may create a large amount of cold, wet compost.

3. Fill a 7.5-10cm (3-4in) wide pot with equal parts moist peat and sharp sand. It is essential that it is well-drained and aerated. Waterlogged compost encourages rotting cuttings.

4. Insert the cutting, then firm the potting compost around it. The lower 36-50mm (1-2in) should be buried in the compost. Water the compost and allow excess to drain.

5. To encourage rapid rooting, place the pot and cutting in an opaque bag and place in gentle warmth. Inspect the compost every ten days to ensure it has not become dry. When shoots appear, remove the bag and slowly acclimatise the plant to a lower temperature and less humidity. When the pot is full of roots, transfer it to a larger pot.

Cane cuttings are used to increase several thick-stemmed houseplants, such as yuccas, dracaenas and dieffenbachias. These are plants that often lose their lower leaves. Chopping up stems to form cuttings obviously destroys a plant – especially with yuccas, cordylines and dracaenas – but does eventually create several others. Dieffenbachias, however, usually have several stems and the removal of just one to form cuttings does not destroy the plant. Spring and early summer are the best times to take and root these cuttings. There are two types of cane cuttings: those laid horizontally on the potting compost, and ones that are inserted vertically.

Horizontal cane cuttings of Dieffenbachias, dracaenas and cordylines can be increased in this way.

1. Sever a strong and healthy stem at its base, trying not to spoil the plant's shape. However, sometimes it is better to use the entire plant as cuttings than to nurse the unsightly remains.

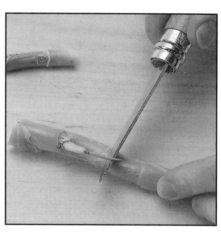

2. Use a sharp knife to cut the stems into 5-7.5cm (2-3in) lengths, each having at least one strong and healthy bud. These buds grow from the old leaf-joints (nodes).

3. Fill and firm a pot with equal parts moist peat and sharp sand. Press each cutting – the bud facing upwards – to half its thickness in the compost, and secure with pieces of bent wire.

4. Water lightly, allow to drain and insert small pieces of split cane around the pot's edge. Place a plastic bag over the pot. Alternatively, use a plastic dome. Place in gentle warmth.

Bulbs and corms are miracles of the plant world. They are store houses of flower power, remaining dormant for long periods then bursting into growth and colour after being given a cold period followed by gentle warmth. In Nature, most bulbs burst into flower in spring. But if they are exposed to cool periods in autumn and early winter, then given warmth, early flowering is encouraged. Also, some bulbs are specially treated by bulb specialists to encourage early flowering. These are known as 'special-prepared' bulbs. Few bulbous plants are as stately – or sweetly-scented – as Hyacinths. Never mix varieties in the same bowl, as they seldom flower at the same time.

1. Plant healthy, equally-sized bulbs of the same variety in a clean, 18-23cm (7-9in) wide bulb bowl. Half fill with damp bulb-fibre or potting compost, then position one bulb in the centre.

2. Place other bulbs around the central one, spacing them 12mm (^{1}/4in) apart. When planted, the noses of the bulbs must be above the surface of the potting compost.

3. Use your fingers to pack bulb-fibre or potting compost firmly – but not rammed – around the bulbs. When completed, the potting mixture should be 12mm (^{1}/4in) below the pot's rim.

4. Water the potting mixture thoroughly with a fine-rosed watering-can, allowing excess to drain. Place the pot in a cool, dark, vermin-proof place to encourage the development of roots.

5. Put the pot in a black polythene bag and place in a cool cellar or shed. Or put outside on a firm surface, against a north-facing wall, and cover with 20cm (8in) of moist peat, then black polythene.

6. When the roots are well developed and the shoots 5-7.5cm (2-3in) above the compost, move the pot to a cool position indoors. Keep the potting compost moist. Do not exceed 10°C/50°F.

1. In late summer, fill a bulb-glass with clean water so that when a bulb is placed on top its base is just covered. Do not overfill with water, as the base of the bulb will then rot. Place in a cool, dark, frost-free cellar or garage until roots have grown about 10cm (4in) long and the shoots are 2.5cm (1in) out of the neck of the bulb. Regularly check the water level.

2. When the shoots and roots have developed, move the bulb-glass into a cool position indoors. Slowly increase the temperature to 18°C/64°F. Keep the water level with the bulb's base.

▲ An unusual and eye-catching way to grow hyacinths for Christmas is in bulb-glasses (modern ones are made of plastic). They resemble hour-glasses, the upper part holding a bulb and the lower half acting as a water reservoir.

Daffodils are types of Narcissus, distinguished by having large central tubes, known as trumpets, which are at least as long as one of the petals. All others are broadly known as narcissi. Both types are grown in pots for flowering indoors, creating attractive arrangements. Early flowering is encouraged by planting 'specially-prepared' bulbs, which can be bought at most florists.

1. In late summer, pot up healthy bulbs in clean, well-drained, 18-23cm (7-9in) wide pots containing damp bulb-fibre or potting compost. Half fill the bowl with one of these potting mixtures.

2. Place the bulbs close together, with their noses about level with the container's rim. This will ensure that they are at about the correct height after the potting mixture has been added.

3. Pack bulb-fibre or potting compost around each bulb, gently working it between them. Eventually, the surface of the potting mixture should be 12mm ($^1/_4$in) below the container's rim.

4. Thoroughly water the potting mixture to settle it around each bulb. To encourage the development of roots the pot must be placed in a cool, dark, vermin-proof place. Put the pot in a black polythene bag and place in a cool cellar or shed. Or put outside on a firm surface, against a north-facing wall, and cover with 20cm (8in) of moist peat, then black polythene. Leave the bulbs for 12 to 15 weeks, until shoots are 10cm (4in) high. Then take indoors, slowly increasing the temperature from 7°C/45°F to 15°C/60°F. Keep the potting mixture moist.

Brightly-faced crocuses (Crocus chrysanthus) flower outdoors in late winter and spring. They can also be encouraged to flower indoors, slightly earlier. However, they cannot be forced in the same way as daffodils and tulips – high temperatures soon kill them. The normal Crocus chrysanthus types are better for growing indoors than the large-flowered hybrids. Handle the corms with care – avoid snapping off young shoots. Pot up in late summer for flowering indoors in late winter. Use shallow pots, as well as special crocus bowls with holes in their sides.

In late summer, pot up top-sized corms, using bulb compost. Space the corms 18mm ($^3/_4$in) apart and 5cm (2in) deep. Also position some to grow out through the holes in the sides of the pot. Lightly water the compost. Place the pot in a black polythene bag. Regularly check that the potting compost is moist.

▼ When shoots are about 2.5cm (1in) high, move the pot indoors into a cool position. Keep the potting compost moist and do not exposed to high temperatures.

Several tulips are suitable for forcing to flowers in spring including 'Early Single' and 'Early Double' types. Plant in late summer or early autumn for flowering from mid winter to mid-spring. For early flowering plant 'specially- prepared' bulbs as soon as they are available in late summer.

1. In late summer place bulbs close together and deep enough so that their noses will be below the surface of the potting mixture, itself 12mm (^{1}/4in) below the container's rim.

2. Use your fingers to spread and firm the potting mixture between and over the bulbs. Unlike hyacinths and daffodils, tulip bulbs must be covered with the potting mixture.

3. Thoroughly water the potting mixture. To encourage root development, place the container in a cool, dark, vermin-proof area. Put the pot in a black polythene bag and place in a cool cellar or shed. Or put outside on a firm surface, against a north-facing wall and cover with 20cm (8in) of moist peat, then black polythene.

4. Between 14 and 16 weeks later shoots will be about 5cm (2in) high. Move indoors to 7-10°F/45-50°C. When the foliage is 10cm (4in) high gradually increase to 18°C/64°F. Keep the potting compost or bulb-fibre moist.

Often known as Amaryllis and related to the bulbous Belladonna Lily (Amaryllis belladonna, a tender garden bulb), Hippeastrums create large, funnel-shaped flowers at the tops of stiff stems. Bulbs planted in late summer and early autumn flower in late winter and spring. However, specially-prepared bulbs if planted in autumn will flower at Christmas and the New Year. Additionally, there arc types that can be planted in early spring for flowering in summer and autumn.

1. Pot up bulbs individually into 13-15cm (6in) wide pots. Use potting compost and leave half of the bulb exposed. Water the potting compost thoroughly and place in 13-16°C/55-61°F.

2. Keep the compost lightly moist until shoots appear, then increase the frequency of watering. When the bulb is growing strongly, feed at weekly intervals with a weak liquid fertilizer. After the flowers fade, continue to water and apply a weekly feed until leaves become yellow. Then, stop feeding and watering and allow the bulb – still in its pot – to dry. Repot the bulb every year, giving it fresh potting compost.

Many small houseplants can be grown in a wide range of glass containers, mainly carboys but also ornate and unusually-shaped bottles and glass domes. There are many plants to choose from, for both 'stoppered' and 'unstoppered' containers. Flowering plants, as well as large, fast-growing, hairy-surfaced or soft-leaved types are unsuitable for stoppered containers.

Traditionally, bottle gardens once planted were 'stoppered' and the moisture and air inside recycled by the plants. In recent years, however, many other containers have been used, some left open to the air.

With 'stoppered' containers it is essential to achieve the correct degree of moisture in the compost – the critical factor when creating a bottle garden.

After planting, wait a day before putting on the stopper to allow excess moisture to escape. If, after the top is put on, the inside becomes misted but clears by midday, the moisture content is correct and it can be left closed.

However, if vast amounts of moisture collects on the inside of the glass, there is too much water and the top must be left off for a couple of days. Conversely, if after planting, watering and being stoppered no moisture appears on the glass, the compost is too dry and needs a further watering.

1. Form a 2.5cm (1in) thick layer of gravel chippings, then a thin layer of charcoal, in the base. Use a funnel formed of cardboard to add a 5cm (2in) thick layer of potting compost.

2. Remove plants from their pots and tease out roots. Start planting from the centre outwards. If the opening is narrow, use spoons and forks tied to short canes to manipulate them.

3. To make the surface of the potting compost more attractive, sprinkle an even layer of either well-washed shingle or expanded clay particles over the surface. Do not cover the plants.

4. Lightly water the compost by dribbling water down the inside of the glass. This is better than splashing water over the plants, which may then encourage the onset of decay in some plants.

5. As plants grow, invasive ones may need trimming to prevent the container becoming like a jungle. Use sharp scissors, or a razor-blade attached to a cane, to cut back long stems.

Also known as terrariums, these are glass cases that, like carboys and other enclosed glass containers, create a humid atmosphere. Early ones resembled rectangular fish tanks, but recent designs are more ornate and in a variety of sizes and interesting shapes. Leaded-glass terrariums are very attractive and when filled with plants create eye-catching features. Planting and caring for them is easier than when in a carboy, and for this reason the range of suitable plants is wider.

Terraria are available in a wide range of sizes and shapes. They are ideal for decorating warm rooms where the light is filtered and gentle. Shapes range from square and round-ended greenhouses to pagodas. Some have removable roofs, enabling easy planting and care of the plants, while others have removable side panels. Avoid terraria with stained or highly embellished glass.

1. Mark out the area of the terrarium on a piece of card or paper, then arrange the plants on it until a pleasing combination is formed. Use one or two tall plants to create height. Before planting, ensure the plants are clean. Wipe smooth-leaved plants with a damp cloth, while hairy-leaved types are best cleaned with a soft brush. Dirty plants will mar the display.

2. Spread a 18mm (³/₄ in) layer of washed gravel over the terrarium's base, then a thin layer of charcoal and 5cm (2in) of loam-based potting compost. Ensure the compost is damp.

3. Starting at one end, make a depression in the potting compost and set the plant in position, firming soil around it. It is usually necessary first to tease and spread out the plant's roots.

4. While setting the plants in position it is likely that the inside of the glass will become dirty. This can be removed by tying a piece of sponge to a small cane, then wiping the glass.

5. Mist-spray smooth-leaved plants and lightly dampen the surface of the potting compost. Avoid swamping it with water. Close all apertures and leave the terrarium for a few days.

6. If vast amounts of condensation builds up on the inside of the glass, it indicates that the potting compost is too wet. Leave an aperture open for a day to remove excess moisture.

Displaying houseplants in indoor hanging-baskets needs care and planning. They attractively fill vertical space but can be difficult to water and look after. Also, they need firm securing points. Although similar to outdoor hanging-baskets, indoor types must be fitted with drip trays to ensure excess water does not fall on carpets. In conservatories with tiled floors this is not so important. Alternatively, plants can be left in their pots and placed in a wide, large pot that does not have a hole in its base. This is then suspended in an attractive harness. Both flowering and foliage trailing plants can be used; if the position is shaded, use only shade-surviving foliage plants, whereas bright and sunny places can be filled with flowering types.

1. Plan the positioning of individual plants before setting them in the basket. Draw a circle the size of the container on a piece of paper and arrange the plants.

2. Form a thin layer of gravel in the container's base to ensure water can run freely into the drip tray. If there are just a few large holes, place broken pieces of clay pots over them.

3. Cover the base with peat-based potting compost, to which has been added a handful of charcoal to prevent it becoming sour. The addition of clay particles helps in moisture retention.

4. Remove the pots and first plant in the centre of the container, packing potting compost around and between each plant. Ensure each plant has been watered several hours earlier.

5. When planting trailing and cascading plants, slightly tilt them around the outside of the container, so that their stems are able to hang freely and therefore cascade attractively.

Instead of removing plants from their pots and planting them in potting compost, plants can be stood in an ornamental pot (without a hole in its base) and suspended in an ornamental harness. The advantage of this method is that the display can be changed as soon as one of the plants stops flowering or becomes unsightly. Flowering houseplants with short seasons of flower can be displayed in this way.

1. Draw a circle the same size as the bowl on a sheet of paper and place the plants on it. It is not necessary to create a congested group – a few distinctive plants can be equally attractive.

2. Select a wide, flat-based bowl 20-25cm (8-10in) wide and 13-15cm (5-6in) deep. Form a 2.5cm (1in) thick layer of pea-shingle in the base to prevent the pots standing in water if excessively watered. Water the plants, allow to drain and position them in the bowl. Packing moist peat between the pots helps to keep them cool and to reduce the amount of water they need.

3. Sphagnum moss placed around the edges makes the display more attractive. However, it is essential the compost can be seen as the plants must be watered individually.

▶ Keeping the plants in their pots means that the display is quick-and-easy to make, and also means you can quickly change one plant in the display for another.

Also known as hydroponics and soil-less culture, hydroculture is an interesting and exciting way to grow houseplants. It involves growing plants with their roots in a nutrient solution instead of a potting compost. It is an ideal way to grow houseplants if they are likely to be neglected for long periods. It is more expensive to grow houseplants in this way, although they do not need as much regular maintenance. As long as an occasional check is made to ensure that the water level is correct, there is no risk of giving your plant either too much or too little water. Also, plants are always given the right amount of chemicals to keep them healthy.

1. Carefully remove the soil-ball by inverting the plant and tapping the pot's edge on a firm surface, supporting the soil-ball with one hand and removing the pot with the other.

2. Immerse the soil-ball in a bowl of lukewarm, clean water and gently wash away the potting compost. Ensure that all soil is removed, even from between very small and fine roots.

3. Use sharp scissors to cut away damaged roots, as well as brown ones. Also, trim back long roots. To keep the size of foliage in balance with the extent of the roots, trim back a few shoots.

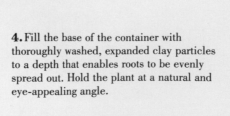

4. Fill the base of the container with thoroughly washed, expanded clay particles to a depth that enables roots to be evenly spread out. Hold the plant at a natural and eye-appealing angle.

5. Continue to dribble washed clay particles around the roots until slightly below the rim of the container. Coloured stones placed one-third up the glass jar create additional interest.

6. Place large pebbles on top of the clay particles and pour in clean tap water at room temperature to cover the roots. Place in shade until plants are established and growing strongly.

Plant Guide

The range of houseplants is wide and each year new species and varieties are introduced and sold through garden centres and nurseries. Some are grown for their attractive foliage, others for their brightly coloured flowers, while a few have colourful berries.

▲ Begonia Limmingheana (Shrimp Begonia)

Many flowering houseplants have a trailing and cascading nature that enables them to be grown in indoor hanging-baskets, in pots placed in wall-brackets, or positioned at the edges of shelves. Ensure that the plants are placed where they can be regularly watered and are not continually knocked by people walking near them.

Easy to grow
* Aporocactus flagelliformis (syn. Cereus flagelliformis) Rat's Tail Cactus/Rattail Cactus.
Funnel-shaped, 7.5cm (3in) long, magenta flowers in mid and late spring.
Propagation: Cuttings and Seeds.

* Campanula isophylla Falling Stars/Italian Bellflower/Star of Bethlehem.
Star-shaped, 2.5cm (1in) wide, blue flowers in mid and late summer. 'Alba' has white flowers.
Propagation: Seeds and Cuttings.

* Schizocentron elegans (syn. Heterocentron elegans) Spanish Shawl.
Saucer-shaped, 2.5cm (1in) wide, rose-purple flowers in summer.
Propagation: Cuttings.

Plants needing care
* Begonia limmingheana (syn. Begonia glaucophylla) Shrimp Begonia.
Clusters of 2.5cm (1in) wide, coral-red flowers in winter. Glossy leaves up to 13cm (5in) long.
Propagation: Cuttings.

* Begonia tuberhybrida pendula Basket Begonia.

Pendent, 5-7.5cm (2-3in) wide flowers in a range of colours from early to late summer.
Propagation: Cuttings and Division of tubers.

* Pelargonium peltatum Hanging Geranium/Ivy Geranium/Ivy-leaved Geranium.
Star-shaped, 2.5cm (1in) wide, flowers in a wide colour range from late spring to early autumn.
Propagation: Cuttings.

* Rhipsalidopsis gaertneri (syn. Schlumbergera gaertneri) Easter Cactus.
Bell-shaped, 36mm ($1^1/4$)in wide, bright red flowers during early and mid spring. Each flower has sharply-pointed petals.
Propagation: Cuttings.

* Saintpaulia grotei Trailing African Violet.
Five-petalled, violet-like flowers,

▲ Columnea x banksii (Stavanger)

2.5cm (1in) wide, in several colours from early to late summer.
Propagation: Leaf-petiole cuttings.

* Schlumbergera 'Buckleyi' (syn. S. hybrida) Christmas Cactus.
Narrowly trumpet-shaped, 5-7.5cm (2-3in) long, magenta or rose-coloured flowers from early winter to late winter.
Propagation: Cuttings.

* Schlumbergera truncata (syn. Zygocactus truncatus) Claw Cactus/Crab Cactus /Linkleaf/Thanksgiving Cactus/Yoke Cactus.
Narrowly trumpet-shaped, 5-7.5cm (2-3in) long, pink to deep red flowers, from late autumn to mid winter. The flat and jointed leaves have deeply incised edges.
Propagation: Cuttings.

Plants with a challenge
* Aeschynanthus radicans (syn. Aeschynanthus pulcher/

Trichosporum lobbianum)
Lipstick Vine.
Tubular and hooded, 36mm ($1^1/2$in) long, crimson flowers during late spring and early summer.
Propagation: Cuttings and Layering.

* Aeschynanthus speciosus (syn. Trichosporum speciosum)
Lipstick Vine.
Tubular and lipped, 5-6.5cm ($2-2^1/2$in) long, bright orange flowers from mid to late summer.
Propagation: Cuttings and Layering.

* Columnea x banksii Goldfish Plant.
Hooded, 6.5-7.5cm ($2^1/2$-3in) long, orange-red flowers from late autumn to mid spring.
Propagation: Cuttings.

* Columnea gloriosa Goldfish Plant.
Hooded, 5-6.5cm ($2-2^1/2$in) long, bright scarlet flowers from early autumn to mid spring.
Propagation: Cuttings

* Columnea microphylla Goldfish Plant.
Hooded, 3.6-5cm ($1^1/2$-2in) long, bright orange-scarlet flowers from late autumn to mid spring.
Propagation: Cuttings.

* Episcia cupreata Flame Violet.
Tubular, 18mm ($1/2$in) wide, orange-red flowers with yellow eyes, amidst 5-10cm (2-4in) long, coppery leaves with silver veins and covered with white hairs.
Propagation: Layering.

* Episcia dianthiflora (syn. Alsobia dianthiflora) Lace Flower/Lace Flower Vine.
Tubular, 36mm (1in) wide, white flowers with feathered edges during summer.
Propagation: Layering.

* Hoya bella Miniature Wax Flower.
Star-shaped, sweetly-scented white flowers with purple or rose-crimson centres and borne in 5cm (2in) wide clusters from late spring to late summer.
Propagation: Cuttings.

▲ Hoya bella (Minature Wax Plant)

Twining stems, richly embroidered with colourful flowers, bring interest to rooms as well as greenhouses and conservatories. Some are vigorous and need the roof of a greenhouse or conservatory to reveal their full beauty, while others happily grow in small pots indoors.

Easy to grow

* Achimenes hybrida Cupid's Bower/Hot Water Plant/Monkey-faced Pansy/Widow's Tears/Mother's Tears.
Trumpet-like, about 36mm ($1^1/_2$ in) wide, in many colours from early summer to early autumn.
Propagation: Cuttings, Seeds and Division of tubers in spring.

* Thunbergia alata Black-eyed Susan.
Tubular, 5cm (2in) wide, orange-yellow flowers with dark centres, from early to late summer.
Propagation: Seeds.

Plants needing care

* Allamanda cathartica 'Grandiflora' Common Allamanda/Golden Trumpet.
Trumpet-shaped and tubular, 7.5cm (3in) wide, bright yellow flowers from mid to late summer.
Propagation: Cuttings.

* Bougainvillea 'Mrs. Butt' Paper Flower.
Papery, 2.5cm (1in) wide, rose-crimson flowers in late summer and early autumn.
Propagation: Cuttings.

* Bouganvillea glabra Paper Flower.
Papery, 2.5cm (1in) wide, flowers in shades of purple and red in late summer and early autumn.
Propagation: Cuttings.

▲ Stephanotis floriabunda (Madagascar Jasmine).

▲ Allamanda carthartica (Golden Trumpet).

▲ Jasminum mesnyi (Japanese Jasmine).

* Clerodendrum thomsoniae
Bag Flower/Bleeding Heart/Glory
Flower/Tropical Bleeding.
Lantern-like, 2.5cm (1in) long,
white flowers with red tips, from
early to late summer.
Propagation: Cuttings.

* Gloriosa rothschildiana climbing
Lily/Flame Lily/Gloriosa Lily/Glory
Lily.
Turk's-cap-like, 10cm (4in) long,
red and yellow flowers during early
and mid summer.
Propagation: Seeds and Division of
tubers in early spring.

* Gloriosa superba Climbing
Lily/Flame Lily/Gloriosa Lily/Glory
Lily.
Turk's-cap-like, 10cm (4in) long,
orange and red flowers during early
and mid summer.
Propagation: Seeds and Division of
tubers in early spring.

* Jasminum mesnyi (syn. Jasminum
primulinum) Japanese Jasmine

/Primrose Jasmine/Yellow Jasmine.
Semi-double, 5cm (2in) wide,
yellow flowers from early to late
spring.
Propagation: Cuttings.

* Jasminum polyanthum Pink
Jasmine.
Star-shaped, 2.5cm (1in) wide,
white and pale pink flowers from
early autumn to late spring.
Propagation: Cuttings.

* Passiflora caerulea Blue Passion
Flower/Common Passion Flower.
Highly ornate and intricate,
7.5cm (3in) wide, white and bluish-
purple flowers from mid to late
summer.
Propagation: Cuttings.

* Plumbago auriculata (syn.
Plumbago capensis) Cape Leadwort.
Star-faced and tubular, 2.5cm (1in)
wide, pale blue flowers from early
summer to autumn.
Propagation: Cuttings.

Plants with a challenge
* Dipladenia sanderi 'Rosea' (syn.
Mandevilla sanderi 'Rosea') Pink
Allamanda.
Trumpet-shaped, 7.5cm (3in) wide,
pink flowers with yellow throats,
from early to late summer.
Propagation: Cuttings.

* Hoya carnosa Honey Plant/Wax
Plant.
Star-shaped, white to flesh-pink
flowers borne in upturned umbrellas
from late spring to late summer.
Propagation: Cuttings.

* Stephanotis floribunda
Floradora/Madagascar Jasmine/Wax
Flower.
Tubular, 36mm (1in) long, white
flowers from late spring to early
autumn.
Propagation: Cuttings.

These are attractive throughout the year. Many are superb for creating permanent and attractive features in sunrooms and conservatories, while others are ideal in rooms, perhaps trailing from indoor hanging-baskets, in pots positioned in wall-brackets or at the edges of shelves.

Easy to grow

* Asparagus densiflorus 'Meyeri' (syn. Asparagus meyeri) Foxtail Fern/Plume Asparagus.
Bright green, needle-like leaves clustered around plume-like stems up to 45cm (1ft) long.
Propagation: Seeds and Division.

* Asparagus densiflorus 'Sprengeri' (syn. Asparagus sprengeri) Asparagus Fern/Emerald Feather/Emerald Fern.
Wiry, trailing stems with bright green, needle-like leaves clustered around them.
Propagation: Seeds and Division.

* Callisia elegans Striped Inch Plant.
Spear-shaped, stem-clasping leaves, 2.5-3.6cm (1-1^1/$_2$in) long, dull green and striped white on their uppersides. Deep purple below.
Propagation: Cuttings.

* Chlorophytum comosum Ribbon Plant/Spider Ivy/Spider Plant /Walking Anthericum.
Long, narrow leaves, often 30cm (12in) or more long, with white and green stripes.
Propagation: Plantlets and Division.

* Ficus pumila Climbing Fig /Creeping Fig/Creeping Rubber Plant.
Heart-shaped, dark green, 2.5cm (1in) long leaves with

▲ Zebrina pendula (Silver Inch Plant).

prominent viens.
Propagation: Cuttings and Layering.

* Nephrolepis exaltata 'Bostoniensis' Boston Fern.
Sword-like, arching fronds, wider than the normal species.
Propagation: Division.

* Oplismenus hirtellus Basket Vine.
Narrow, wavy-edged, stem-clasping leaves, about 7.5cm (3in) long, with

irregular white, pink and green stripes.
Propagation: Cuttings and Division.

* Plectranthus coleoides 'Marginalis' Variegated Candle Flower.
Oval, hairy-surfaced light green, scallop-edged leaves with broad, white edges.
Propagation: Cuttings and Division.

▲ Saxifraga stolonifera (Tricolour - Mother of Thousands).

* Plectranthus oertendahlii
Brazilian Coleus/Swedish Ivy.
Oval to circular, scallop-edged,
green leaves with prominent white
veins.
Propagation: Cuttings and Division.

* Saxifraga stolonifera 'Tricolor'
(syn. Saxifraga sarmentosa
'Tricolor') Creeping Sailor/Magic
Carpet/Mother of
Thousands/Strawberry
Begonia/Strawberry Geranium.
Circular, light green leaves
variegated pink and pale yellow.
Propagation: Plantlets and Division.

* Setcreasea pallida 'Purple Heart'
Purple Heart.
Lance-like and stem-clasping, rich
purple leaves up to 15cm (6in) long.
Propagation: Division.

* Soleirolia soleirolii (syn. Helxine
solcirolii)Angel's Tears/Baby's
Tears/Carpet Plant/Corsican Carpet
Plant/Irish Moss/Mind-Your-Own-
Business.
Small, round, pale to mid-green
leaves densely clustered around
thin, trailing, pink stems.
Propagation: Division.

Plants needing care
* Ceropegia woodii Hearts
Entangled/Hearts-on-a-string
/Rosary Vine/String of Hearts.
Heart-shaped, fleshy, dark green
leaves, 18mm ($^{1}/_{2}$in) long, blotched
with silver.
Propagation: Seeds and Division but
avoid damaging the tubers.

▲ Asparagus densiflorus (Sprengeri).

▲ Chlorophytum comosum (Spider plant).

* Epipremnum pinnatum 'Aureum'
(syn. Epipremnum aureum/Pothos
aureus/Rhaphidophora
aurea/Scindapsus aureus) Devil's
Ivy/Golden Pothos/Pothos Vine/Taro
Vine.
Heart-shaped, 10-13cm (4-5in)
long, green leaves with yellow
blotches. There are several
variegated varieties.
Propagation: Cuttings.

* Gynura aurantiaca Purple Passion
Vine.
Triangular, 10-13cm (4-5in) long,
dark green leaves smothered with
purplish hairs.
Propagation: Cuttings.

* Gynura procumbens (syn. Gynura
sarmentosa) Velvet Plant.
Triangular, 10cm (4in) long, dark
green leaves covered with purplish
hairs.
Propagation: Cuttings.

* Peperomia scandens 'Variegata'
Cupid Peperomia.
Heart-shaped, waxy-surfaced, 5cm
(2in) long, green leaves with yellow
edges.
Propagation: Cuttings.

* Senecio rowleyanus String of
Beads.
Grape-like, glaucous-green leaves
on thread-like trailing stems.
Propagation: Trailing stems root
readily.

Plants with a challenge
* Fittonia verschaffeltii Mosaic
Plant/Painted Leaf Leaf/Silver
Nerve/Silver Net Plant.
Oval leaves, about 5cm (2in) long,
with pink veins.
Propagation: Division.

* Fittonia verschaffeltii
'Argyroneura' (syn. Fittonia
argyroneura) Nerve Plant/Silver Net
Leaf.
Oval, green leaves, about 5cm (2in)
long, with white veins.
Propagation: Division. Trailing
stems root readily.

* Fittonia verschaffeltii
'Argyroneura Nana' (syn. Fittonia
argyroneura nana) Snakeskin Plant.
Oval, green leaves, about 2.5cm
(1in) long, with white veins.
Propagation: Division. Trailing
stems root readily.

Large and dominant foliage plants can become permanent features indoors, often creating eye-catching focal points. Some, such as large palms, are superb when seen against a white background, while others are densely covered in leaves and better when forming screens.

Easy to grow
* Cyperus alternifolius Umbrella Grass/Umbrella Palm/Umbrella Plant/ Umbrella Sedge.
Narrow, grass-like bracts in umbrella-like heads.
Propagation: Seeds and Division.

* X Fatshedera lizei Fat-headed Lizzie/Ivy-tree/Miracle Plant.

▼ Monstera deliciosa (Swiss Cheese Plant).

Deep, shiny green, five-lobed leaves up to 18cm (7in) long.
Propagation: Cuttings.

* Fatsia japonica False Castor Oil Plant/Formosa Rice Tree/Glossy-leaved Paper Plant/Japanese Aralia/Japanese Fatsia/Paper Plant.
Deeply-lobed, glossy-green leaves, often 30cm (12in) wide on mature plants.
Propagation: Seeds and detachment of sucker-like shoots in spring.

* Grevillea robusta Silk Oak/Silky Oak.
Finely dissected, mid to deep green leaves.
Propagation: Seeds.

* Yucca aloifolia Dagger Plant/Spanish Bayonet.
Narrow, stiff and tough leaves.
Propagation: Cane cuttings and

removal and rooting of offsets.

* Yucca elephantipes Spineless Yucca.
Narrow, stiff, tough, rough-edged leaves up to 90cm (3ft) long.
Propagation: Cane cuttings and removal and rooting of offsets.

Plants needing care
* Araucaria heterophylla (syn. A. excelsa) Australian Pine/House Pine/Norfolk Island Pine/Conifer.
Awl-shaped, bright green needles borne on tiered branches.
Propagation: Seeds.

* Ardisia crenata (syn. A. crispa/A. crenulata) Coral Berry/Spice Berry.
Lance-like, stiff, wavy-edged, dark green leaves.
Propagation: Seeds.

* Brassaia actinophylla (syn. Schefflera actinophylla) Umbrella Plant/Umbrella Tree.
Oval to oblong, glossy, mid-green leaflets. These are arranged in threes or fives at the ends of leaf-stalks.
Propagation: Seeds.

* Dizygotheca elegantissima (syn. Aralia elegantissima) False Aralia/Finger Aralia.
Propagation: Seeds.

* Ficus benjamina Benjamin Tree/Java Fig/Small-leaved Rubber Plant/Weeping Fig.
Elliptic and pointed, 10cm (4in) long, dark green leaves, soft green when young.
Propagation: Cuttings.

* Ficus deltoidea (syn F. diversifolia) Mistletoe Fig/ Mistletoe Rubber Fig.
Pear-shaped, leathery, dark green leaves.
Propagation: Cuttings

* Ficus elastica Assam Rubber/ India Rubber Tree/ Rubber Plant.
Oval and wide, leathery, 25-30cm (10-12in) long shiny dark green leaves.
Propagation: Air layering.

* Ficus lyrata Fiddleback Fig/Fiddleleaf Fig.
Fiddle-shaped, wavy-edged, glossy, dark green leaves up to 38cm (15in) long.
Propagation: Air layering and Cuttings.

* Howeia belmoreana (syn. Howea belmoreana/Kentia belmoreana) Belmore Sentry Palm/Curly Palm/Sentry Palm.
Narrow and pointed, dark green leaflets that create leaves 45cm (18in) by 30cm (12in).
Propagation: Seeds.

* Howeia forsteriana (syn. Howea forsteriana/Kentia forsteriana).
Forster Sentry Palm/Kentia Palm/Paradise Palm/Thatch-leaf Palm.

▲ Ficus elastica (Rubber Plant).

▲ Brassaia actinophylla (Umbrella Plant).

Narrow and pointed, dark green leaflets – wider than with H. forsteriana. Similar to Howeia belmoreana, although the leaflets are drooping but fewer of them.
Propagation: Seeds.

* Monstera deliciosa (syn. Philodendron pertusum) Fruit Salad Plant/Hurrican Plant/Split-leaf Philodendron/Swiss Cheese Plant.
Shiny green, up to 45cm/18in wide, leaves with deep indentations along the sides of mature leaves. Juvenile leaves have entire edges.
Propagation: Cuttings.

* Phoenix canariensis Canary Date Palm/Canary Island Date.
Straight and stiff, mid-green leaflets.
Propagation: Seeds.

* Schefflera arboricola (syn. Heptapleurum arboricola) Parasol Plant.
Oval to oblong, pointed, glossy-green leaflets borne in groups of nine at the ends of leaf-stalks.
Propagation: Seeds.

Plants with a challenge
* Dracaena deremensis Dragon Tree
Sword-like leaves up to 45cm (18in) long, glossy green with two longitudinal silvery-white stripes. There are several attractive varieties.
Propagation: Cane cuttings and removal and rooting of basal shoots in spring.

Many indoor plants fill houses, greenhouses and conservatories with rich scents. There are scented houseplants for all seasons, many creating heady and sweet bouquets in winter when rich fragrancies are especially welcome. Some scented plants become permanant features, regularly filling a room with scent, while others are temporary and discarded after flowers fade.

There are also plants with leaves that reveal distinctive scents. Chief among these are scented-leaved pelargoniums.

Easy to grow

* Exacum affine Arabian Violet/German Violet/Persian Violet. Saucer-shaped, purple, yellow-centred, sweetly-scented flowers from mid to late summer. The scent is like that of Lily-of-the-Valley.
Propagation: Seeds.

* Hyacinthus orientalis Dutch Hyacinth/Hyacinth.
Wax-like, five-petalled flowers, tightly clustered in spire-like heads, from mid winter to late spring. Sweet, heady and penetrating bouquet.
Propagation: Seeds, but only use fresh bulbs for forcing each year.

Plants needing care

* Ardisia crenata (syn. A. crispa/A. crenulata) Coral Berry/Spice Berry.

Very sweet bouquet to the star-like, creamy-white flowers in early summer.
Propagation: Seeds.

* Cyclamen persicum (Kaori strain) Cyclamen/Florist's Cyclamen/Persian Violet.
Delicate and sweet bouquet to the winter and spring flowers.
Propagation: Seeds.

* Freesia x hybrida (syn. Freesia x kewensis) Freesia.
Very sweet bouquet to the funnel-shaped, mid winter to mid spring, flowers.
Propagation: Seeds and removal of cormlets.

* Jasminum polyanthum Pink Jasmine.

▲ Exacum affine (Persian Violet).

Sweet and penetrating bouquet to the late autumn to mid spring, white and pale pink flowers.
Propagation: Cuttings.

* Nerium oleander Oleander/Rosebay.
Clusters of sweet, single, white flowers from early summer to autumn. Beware of the poisonous sap and wood.
Propagation: Seeds and Cuttings.

* Senecio rowleyanus String of Beads.
Sweetly-scented white flowers from late summer to late autumn.
Propagation: Trailing stems readily root.

▲ Primula x kewensis.

▼ Primula malacoides (Fairy Primrose).

Plants with a challenge
* Cestrum parqui Willow-leaved Jasmine.
Greenish-yellow flowers with a sweet, night fragrance from mid to late summer.
Propagation: Cuttings.

* Gardenia jasminoides Cape Jasmine/Gardenia.

Heavily sweet, 7.5cm (3in) wide white flowers during early and mid-summer.
Propagation: Cuttings.

* Hoya bella Miniature Wax Flower.
Star-shaped, sweetly-scented white flowers in 5cm/2in wide clusters from late spring to late summer.
Propagation: Cuttings.

* Hoya carnosa Honey Plant/Wax Plant.
Sweetly-scented, star-shaped, white to flesh-pink flowers borne in upturned umbrellas from late spring to late summer.
Propagation: Cuttings.

* Pittosporum tobira Australian Paurel/House-blooming Mock Orange/Japanese Pittosporum/Mock Orange.
Creamy-white flowers with an orange fragrance from mid spring to mid summer.
Propagation: Cuttings.

* Stephanotis floribunda Floradora/Madagascar Jasmine/Wax Flower.
Tubular, 36mm ($1^1/2$in) long, white flowers, with a heavily sweet fragrance, from late spring to early autumn.
Propagation: Cuttings.

Insectiverous plants reveal how nature has adapted some plants to live in places where their roots are unable to absorb nutrients. Some, such as the Venus Fly Trap, use hinged jaws to capture insects, others employ sticky surfaces or pitcher-like heads that trap and prevent the escape of insects. They are not easy to grow indoors in a dry atmosphere, and need to be watered with rainwater and kept moist and humid. Take care not to expose them to aerosols.

Plants needing care
* Dionaea muscipula Venus Fly Trap.
Hinged jaws that trap flies. Open jaws close when an insect touches trigger hairs inside them. Digestive juices break down the insect's body and the plant absorbs the nutrients. The jaws eventually re-open to trap further insects.
Propagation: Seeds and Division.

Plants with a challenge
* Darlingtonia californica (syn. Chrysamphora californica) Californian Pitcher Plant/Cobra Lily/Cobra Orchid/Hooded Pitcher Plant.
It has hoods that resemble a cobra's head, heavily-veined, yellowish or pale green and up to 60cm (2ft) high. There is an opening on the underside of each hood, and any insect venturing inside is doomed to become a meal for the plant. Downward-pointing hairs make it difficult for an insect to escape.
Propagation: Seeds and Division.

* Drosera binata (syn. D. dichotoma/D. intermedia) Giant Fork-leaved Sundew.
It gains it name from the way the deeply-lobed leaves divide at their tops into two or four segments. Sticky hairs on the leaves trap and digest insects. White flowers appear at the tops of long stems from early to late summer.
Propagation: Seeds and Division.

▼ Drosera capensis (Sundew).

* Drosera capensis Sundew
Rosettes of leaves covered with red, glandular hairs that both trap and disgest insects. During mid summer purple flowers are borne on stems up to 38cm (15in) high.
Propagation: Seeds and Division.

* Sarracenia x catesbaei Pitcher Plant (syn. Sarracenia hybrida)
A hybrid between S. purpurea and S. flava.
Long, green to dark purple pitchers, with nearly erect lids, veined in purple. During spring, large yellow and purple flowers appear on long, upright and stiff stems.
Propagation: Seeds and Division.

* Sarracenia flava Huntsman's Horn/Trumpet Leaf/Umbrella Trumpets/Watches/Yellow Pitcher Plant.
Long, yellow-green or yellow pitchers, with purple or crimson veining in their throats. Each has an erect lid. Insects fall into a solution of pepsin. In mid and late spring it develops yellow, nodding flowers on long stems.
Propagation: Seeds and Division.

* Sarracenia purpurea Huntsman's-cup/Indian Cup/Pitcher Plant/Side-saddle Flower.
Semi-erect, purple and green pitchers. In spring it develops greenish-purple, nodding flowers on long, erect stems. Like all pitchers plants, insects fall into a pepsin solution, drown and are digested by the plant.
Propagation: Seeds and Division.

▲ Sarracenia flava (Huntman's Horn).

▶ Dionaea muscipula (Venus Fly Trap).

Botanically, fruits are mature ovaries (female part of a flower). They bear ripe seeds and may be soft and fleshy or dry pods. Berries, however, are fleshy and juicy fruits.

To most houseplant enthusiasts these are synonymous and refer to any plant that reveals colourful and attractive berries. They range from bright red berries to orange-like fruits. Do not expect to grow types that can be eaten, as high humidity and temperatures are usually needed. Nevertheless, they bring an attractive and unusual feature to the home.

▲ Solanum capsicastrum (Winter Cherry).

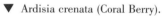
▼ Ardisia crenata (Coral Berry).

Easy to grow
* Nertera depressa (syn. Nertera granadensis/Gomozia granadensis) Bead Plant.
Creeping evergreen with small, oval to rounded, light green leaves. Insignificant greenish-yellow flowers appear in early summer, followed by glossy, bright orange berries during autumn and well into winter.
Propagation: Division.

* Rhipsalis cassutha (syn. R. baccifera).
A member of the Cactaceae family, in the wild trailing for up to 7.5m (25ft) but much less when grown in a small pot indoors. Pale green, cylindrical stems bear creamy flowers in summer, followed by small, round, white fruits.
Propagation: Cuttings.

Plants needing care
* Ardisia crenata (syn. A. crispa/A. crenulata) Coral Berry/Spice Berry.
Shrub-like houseplant with a very sweet bouquet to the star-like, creamy-white flowers in early summer. These are followed by long-lasting, glossy, scarlet berries that crowd on stiff stalks.
Propagation: Seeds.

* Capsicum annuum
Chilli/Christmas Pepper/Green
Pepper/Ornamental Pepper/Red
Pepper.
Short-lived, shrubby perennial
usually treated as an annual and
grown for its decorative, red, green
or yellow fruits that appear during
autumn and into winter.
Fruits range in shape – spherical,
conical with twisted or wrinkled
surfaces.
Propagation: Seeds.

* Ficus deltoidea (syn F.
diversifolia) Mistletoe Fig/Mistletoe
Rubber Fig.

Shrub-like with pear-shaped,
leathery, dark green leaves.
Throughout the year, yellow or dull
red berry-like fruits about
12mm ($^1/_2$ in) long are borne on
long stalks from the upper leaf-
joints.
Propagation: Cuttings.

* Solanum capsicastrum Winter
Cherry.
A half-hardy evergreen shrub that
produces attractive fruits in winter.
Initially, these are marble-like,
slightly-pointed and green, slowly
turning orange-red.
Propagation: Seeds.

Plants with a challenge
* X Citrofortunella mitis (syn.
Citrus mitis Calamondin
Orange/Panama Orange.
Widely-known citrus fruit – usually
sold as Citrus mitis – for growing
indoors, in greenhouses and
conservatories, as it flowers and
bears fruits while still small.
Highly-scented white flowers are
borne throughout the year and
followed by round, 25-36mm
($1-1^1/_2$in) wide, fruits that slowly
change from dark green to orange-
yellow.
Propagation: Cuttings.

* Citrus limon 'Meyeri'(syn. Citrus
meyeri) Chinese Dwarf Lemon/
Dwarf Lemon/Meyer Lemon.
This is a dwarf lemon, ideal as a
houseplant but especially suitable
for growing in greenhouses or
conservatories. It has dark green
leaves and highly scented, red-
flushed, white flowers in spring and
early summer. The fruits are dark
green at first and take many months
to ripen, but don't expect them to be
anything but ornamental.
Propagation: Cuttings.

▲ Capsicum annuum (Christmas Pepper).

▶ X Citrofortunella mitis (Calamondin Orange).

South-facing windowsills are the brightest positions in a home, but can be too bright for some plants. Houseplants suggested here happily live within 60cm (2ft) of windows facing south. However, plants such as desert cacti (types that grow in semi-desert regions and at ground-level), succulent plants and pelargoniums thrive on windowsills.

Easy to grow
* Astilbe japonica Spiraea.
Plume-like, feathery heads of flowers in red, pink or white in late winter and early spring. Do not confuse this plant with garden shrubs in the genus Spiraea.
Propagation: Division.

* Aucuba japonica 'Variegata' (syn. A. japonica 'Maculata') Gold Dust Plant/Gold Dust Tree/Spotted Laurel Lance-like, shiny-green leaves with yellow spots.
Propagation: Cuttings – with heels.

* Cacti (Desert Types).
There are many interestingly-shaped cacti to choose from within this group, including those in families Chamaecereus, Echinopsis, Lobivia, Mammillaria, Notocactus, Parodia and Rebuntia.
Propagation: Seeds and Cuttings.

* Celosia argentea cristata (syn. Celosia cristata)
Cockscomb/Woolflower.
Cock's-comb-like flowers, in shades of red, orange or yellow, from mid to late summer.
Propagation: Seeds.

* Chrysanthemum.
All-year-round year types in pots are available throughout the year. Wide colour range.
Propagation: Cuttings.

* Coleus blumei Flame Nettle/Painted Leaves/Painted Nettle.
Nettle-like leaves in a wide colour range. Plants are widely available in summer.
Propagation: Cuttings and Seeds.

* Daffodils
Large, trumpet-like flowers, mainly in yellow.

▲ Fatsia japonica (False Castor Oil Plant).

Propagation: Bulbils, but use fresh bulbs each year.

* Hippeastrum hybrida Amaryllis/Barbados Lily.
Large, trumpet-shaped flowers at the tops of stiff stems. Some flower in summer and autumn. Wide colour range.
Propagation: Offsets, but use fresh bulbs each year.

* Hyacinthus orientalis Dutch Hyacinth/Hyacinth.
Erect spires of sweetly-scented flowers, mid winter to early spring.
Propagation: Plant fresh bulbs each year.

* Impatiens walleriana (syn. Impatiens holstii) Busy Lizzie/Busy Lizzy/Patient Lucy/ Sultana/ Zanzibar Balsam
Flat-faced, trumpet-like flowers prolifically borne from mid spring to early autumn. Wide colour range.
Propagation: Seeds and Cuttings.

* Iresine herbstii Beefsteak Plant/Blood Leaf.
Notch-topped, oval, wine-red leaves. I. herbstii aureoreticulata, the Chicken Gizzard plant, has yellowish leaves.
Propagation: Cuttings.

* Schizanthus pinnatus Butterfly Flower/Poor Man's Orchid.
Brightly-coloured, orchid-like flowers, marked and spotted, rose, purple and yellow, on bushy plants

▲ Hibiscus rosa-sinensis (Chinese Rose).

▲ Cordyline fructicosa.

in spring or late summer.
Propagation: Seeds.

* Succulents
Many interesting-shaped plants, in families such as Agave, Aloe, Ceropegia, Bryophyllum, Crassula, Echevaria, Euphorbia, Gasteria, Lithops, Sempcrvivum and Sedum.
Propagation: Seeds, Plantlets and Cuttings.

* Tolmiea menziesii Pickaback Plant/Piggyback Plant/Thousand Mothers/Youth-on-age.
Maple-like, bright green leaves. Plantlets grow on the upper surfaces, and can be removed and rooted.
Propagation: Plantlets.

* Tulips
Tulips such as Early Single, Early Double, Darwin and Lily-flowered types can be encouraged to îlower indoors.
Propagation: Use fresh bulbs each year.

Plants needing care
* Codiaeum variegatum pictum Croton/Jacob's Coat/Variegated Laurel.
Colourful, leathery, shiny leaves, variously shaped. Wide range of varieties.
Propagation: Cuttings.

* Cordyline fruticosa (syn. Cordyline terminalis/Draceaena terminalis).
Good Luck Plant/Flaming Dragon Tree/Hawaiin Good Luck Plant/Ti Plant/Tree of Kings.
Palm-like trunk bearing lance-shaped, mid to deep green leaves suffused with red, purple or cream. Several attractive varieties.
Propagation: Cane Cuttings and detaching and repotting sucker-like shoots in spring.

* Euphorbia pulcherrima.
Christmas Flower/Christmas

Star/Lobster Plant/Mexican Flameleaf/Poinsettia.
Brightly-colour bracts clustered at the tops of plants, mainly scarlet but also white or pink. Flowering mainly at Christmas.
Propagation: Cuttings.

* Hibiscus rosa-sinensis.
Blacking Plant/China Rose/Chinese Hibiscus/Rose of China.
Large, trumpet-shaped, pink, red, white, yellow or orange flowers, often 13cm (5in) wide, from early to late summer.
Propagation: Cuttings – with heels.

* Hypoestes phyllostachya (syn. H. sanguinolenta).
Flamingo Plant/Freckle Face/Measles Plant/Pink Dot/Polka-dot Plant.
Dull green leaves irregularly peppered with pink spots.
Propagation: Cuttings.

* Rhododendron simsii Azalea/Indian Azalea.
Tightly packed flowers, in colours including white, orange, pink or red. Plants are encouraged to flower during winter.
Propagation: Cuttings.

* Vallota speciosa (syn. V. purpurea).
Scarborough Lily Cup to trumpet-shaped flowers clustered at the tops of stiff, upright stems from mid to late summer.
Propagation: Removal of offsets when repotting.

Plants with a challenge
* Beloperone guttata (syn. Justicia brandegeana)False Hop/Mexican Shrimp Plant/Shrimp Plant Distinctive, shrimp-like flowers from mid spring to late autumn.
Propagation: Cuttings

◄ Hippeastrum hybrida (Amaryllis).

Some plants are better suited to soft lighting. They should be positioned are between 60cm (2ft) and 1.2m (4ft) from a bright south-facing window, or much closer to a north-facing one. The light is bright, but not created by strong and direct sun rays. Here is a range of plants that will live in these conditions.

Easy to grow
* Begonia masoniana Iron Cross Begonia.
Somewhat triangular and lop-sided, crinkly-surfaced, mid-green leaves prominently embossed with a deep purple-bronze cross.
Propagation: Whole-leaf cuttings, Leaf-squares and Leaf-triangles.

* Begonia rex King Begonia/Painted Leaf Begonia/Rex Begonia.
Somewhat triangular and lop-sided leaves, usually colourfully zoned.
Propagation: Whole-leaf cuttings, Leaf-squares and Leaf-triangles.

* Calceolaria x herbeohybrida (syn. C. x hybrida) Pocketbook

Flower/Pouch Flower/Slipper Flower/Slipperwort.
Distinctive, pouch-like flowers in bright colours, such as yellow, orange, red or white, and peppered and blotched with other colours, from late spring to mid summer.
Propagation: Seeds.

* Kalanchoe blossfeldiana Flaming Katy.
Oval, scalloped-edged, slightly succulent dark green leaves. Tubular, scarlet flowers borne in dense heads, normally from late winter to late spring but plants can be encouraged to flower throughout the year. Varieties in pink, white or yellow.
Propagation: Seeds.

* Pilea microphylla (syn. P. muscosa).
Artillery Plant/Gunpowder Plant Fern-like, bushy plant with yellow-green flowers from late spring to late summer.
Propagation: Cuttings.

* Senecio cruentus (syn. Cineraria cruenta) Cineraria.
Large, colouful, daisy-like flowers in massed heads from early winter

▲ Cissus antarctica (Kangaroo Vine).

to early summer. Varieties in many colours.
Propagation: Seeds.

* Sparmannia africana African Hemp/House Lime.
Heart-shaped, bright green leaves covered with soft hairs. White flowers from late spring to early summer.
Propagation: Cuttings.

Plants needing care
* Aglaoenema modestum Chinese Evergreen.
Long, spear-shaped leaves. Many other species, some with attractively variegated leaves.
Propagation: Division and removal of basal shoots in spring.

* Aphelandra squarrosa Saffron Plant/Zebra Plant.
Oval and pointed, dark green leaves with ivory veins. Cone-shaped heads formed of yellow flowers appear from mid to late summer.
Propagation: Cuttings.

* Dieffenbacia maculata (syn. D. picta) Dumb Cane/Leopard Lily/Spotted Dumb Cane.

▲ Plectranthus coleoides (Marginatus).

Large, oblong leaves in many colours. Avoid contact with the sap. Many colourful varieties.
Propagation: Cane cuttings.

* Bromeliads
Wide range of distinctive plants, many with leaves forming urns, including genera Aechmea, Ananas, Cryptanthus, Guzmania, Neoregelia and Vriesia.
Propagation: Division and removal of offsets.

* Ctenanthe oppenheimiana tricolor Never Never Plant.
Narrow, lance-shaped leaves with dark green and grey bands.
Propagation: Division.

* Maranta leuconeura Prayer Plant/Ten Commandments.
Oval, emerald-green leaves, blotched in purple-brown, that stand upright at night, as if in prayer. Several attractive varieties.
Propagation: Division.

* Pilea cadierei Aluminium Plant/Watermelon Pilea.
Oval and pointed, mid-green, quilted leaves with silvery patches.
Propagation: Cuttings.

* Rhoeo spathacea (syn. Rhoeo discolor).

Fleshy, lance-shaped, glossy-green leaves with purplish undersides.
Propagation: Division and Cuttings from basal shoots in spring.

Plants with a challenge
* Acalypha hispida
Chenille Plant/Fox Tail/Philippine Medusa/Red Cat Tail/Red-hot Catstail.
Long, tail-like stems packed with red flowers during summer and into autumn.
Propagation: Cuttings (pp 42/43).

* Anthurium andreanum
Flamingo Lily/Oilcloth Flower/Painter's Palette.
Large, heart-shaped leaves and waxy red spathes from which arise straight columns of flowers.
Propagation: Division.

* Anthurium crystallinum Crystal Anthurium/Strap Flower.
Large, heart-shaped, velvet-surfaced, dark green leaves with attractive ivory veins.
Propagation: Division.

* Anthurium scherzerianum
Flamingo Flower/Pigtail Anthurium/Pigtail Plant Dark green, lance-shaped leaves and red spathes with curly, orange-red

▲ Ficus lyrata (Fiddle-leaf Fig).

columns.
Propagation: Division.

* Caladium hortulanum Angel's Wings/Elephant's Ears/Mother-in-law Plant.
Large, arrow-shaped, paper-thin leaves with many attractive colours.
Propagation: Remove and pot-up offsets in spring.

* Calathea makoyana (syn. Maranta makoyana) Brain Plant/Cathedral Windows/Peacock Plant.
Oblong, paper-thin leaves, silvery-green above and attractively patterned.
Propagation: Division.

* Pachystachys lutea Lollipop Plant.
Cone-shaped heads of bright yellow flowers from late spring to autumn.
Propagation: Cuttings.

* Spathiphyllum wallisii Peace Lily/Spathe Flower.
Spear-shaped, glossy-green leaves and white, arum-like flowers on long, upright stems from late spring to mid summer.
Propagation: Division.

▲ Hyacinthus orientalis (Hyacinth).

▲ Syngonium podophyllum (Arrowhead Vine).

No plant will indefinitely survive in total shade, although some grow in shade near a sunless window or where the light is just sufficient to enable a newspaper to be read. If a plant appears sickly, move it to better light to encourage recovery.

Because of the inherent difficulties in growing houseplants in little light, those that are difficult to grow cease to be possible options and therefore most are either easy to grow, or present only a slightly degree of difficulty.

Also, some plants that are moderately easy to grow in moderate light become a challenge when the intensity of light falls. Remember that the intensity of light 2.4m (8ft) from a window is only 5-10% of that on a windowsill.

Many of the plants recommended for growing in soft light can also be grown in slight shade for a limited time.

Easy to grow
* Aspidistra elatior Barroom Plant/Cast Iron Plant.
Long, lance-shaped, dark green leaves. The variegated form needs better light than the all-green type.
Propagation: Division.

* Asplenium bulbiferum Hen-and-chicken Fern/King and Queen Fern/Mother Fern/Mother Spleenwort/Parsley Fern.
Finely-cut, mid-green leaves. Small bulbils arise from their upper surfaces, and can be easily rooted.
Propagation: Division and bulbils.

* Cyrtomium falcatum Fishtail Fern/Holly Fern/Japanese Holly Fern.
Holly-like, stiff, glossy, dark-green leaflets.
Propagation: Division.

Plants needing care
* Dracaena fragrans Corn Plant.
Long, sword-like leaves: attractive varieties have white or silver stripes along the green leaves.
Propagation: Cane cuttings and removal and potting up of basal shoots in spring.

* Dracaena marginata Madagascar Dragon Tree.
Narrowly sword-like green leaves with red edges.
Propagation: Cane cuttings and removal and potting up of basal shoots in spring.

▼ Cissus discolor (Begonia Vine).

Glossary

Acaricide: A chemical used to kill parasitic spider mites.

Acid: Refers to soils and composts with a pH below 7.0.

Activator: A chemical product, normally granular or powdered, that speeds up the decay of plant material in a compost heap.

Adventitious roots: Roots appearing in an unusual position, such as on leaves and stems.

Aerial roots: Roots that appear from a stem above soil-level, as with some Ivies (Hedera) and orchids.

Air layering: A method of increasing certain plants by encouraging roots to form on stems.

Alkaline: Refers to soils with a pH above 7.0.

Alpine: Generally refers to any small plant grown in a rock garden or alpine house.

Alternate: Buds or leaves that grow on opposite sides of a stem, not directly opposite one another.

Annual: A plant that completes its life-cycle within one year.

Anthe: Part of a stamen, the male reproductive part of a flower.

Aphid: Perhaps the best-known pest of plants, also called greenfly and blackfly.

Apical: The tip of a branch or shoot.

Aquati: A plant that grows partly or entirely in water.

Areol: A modified sideshoot, resembling a tiny hump, unique to cacti.

Aroi: A plant belonging to the Arum Family and including Anthuriums, Dieffenbachias, Monsteras and Philodendrons.

Asexual: Non-sexual and frequently used to refer to the vegetative propagation of plants, such as by cuttings and division.

Axil: The junction between a leaf and stem, from where sideshoots or flowers may develop.

Axillary: A bud that grows from an axil, later forming a stem and flowers, or just a stem.

Bearded: A petal bearing a tuft or row of long hairs.

Bedding plant: A plant raised and used as a temporary filler in a border.

Biennial: A plant that makes its initial growth one year and flowers the following one.

Bigeneric hybrid: A plant produced by crossing two plants from different genera.

Bleeding: The loss of sap from plants after they have been cut.

Blind: A plant whose growing point has not developed properly.

Bloom: This has two meanings – either a flower or a powdery coating.

Bolting: The premature shooting up to flower of vegetables. Lettuces, beetroot, spinach and radishes are most susceptible.

Bonsai: The art of growing dwarfed shrubs and trees in small containers.

Botrytis: Also known as grey mould, a fungal disease prevalent in badly ventilated, damp sunrooms, greenhouses and conservatories.

Bordeaux mixture: A fungicidal mixture of copper sulphate and lime.

Bottle gardening: Growing plants in enclosed environments created by large glass jars, such as carboys.

Bottom heat: The warming from below of a rooting mixture, rather from above.

Bract: A modified leaf and usually associated with flowers.

Break: The branching of shoots after the removal of a terminal bud.

Bromeliad: A member of the Bromeliaceae family. Many have rosettes of leaves and colourful bracts, and a few are epiphytes.

Bud: A tightly-packed and enclosed immature shoot or flower.
Bulb: A storage organ with a bud-like structure.
Bulbi: An immature and miniature bulb, usually at the base of another bulb.
Cactus: A succulent plant belonging to the Cactaceae family.
Calcicol: A plant that likes lime.
Calcifuge: A plant that does not like lime.
Calyx: The sepals as a whole; the outer ring of a flower.
Capillary action: The passage of water upwards through soil or potting compost.
Carboy: A large, somewhat round or pear-shaped, glass bottle used as a container for plants.
Catch crop: A crop – usually of a salad nature and sometimes raised in greenhouses – that is sown, grown and harvested while situated between long-growing crops.
Chestnut compound: A mixture of copper sulphate and ammonium carbonate to control some fungal diseases.
Chlorophyll: The green pigment present in all plants, except for a few parasites and fungi.
Chlorosis: A disorder mainly of leaves, with parts becoming light-coloured or whitish.
Cloche: The French for a bell-glass, but now widely used for glass and plastic tunnel-like structures used to protect early-maturing crops, usually vegetables.
Cladode: A modified, flattened stem which takes the form and function of a leaf
Clone: A plant raised vegetatively from another plant, so that it is identical in every particular to other plants raised from the same plant.
Columnar: A plant that rises vertically – usually used to refer to trees and conifers, but also to describe some cacti.
Compost: Has two meanings. The first refers to the medium in which plants grow when in pots or other containers, and in North America is known as potting soil.
Compound leaf: A leaf formed of two or more leaflets. Compound leaves are characterized by not having buds in the axils of their leaflets.
Corm: An underground storage organ formed of a greatly swollen stem base, suchas a gladiolus.

Corolla: The ring of petals in a flower, creating the main display.
Corona: The development of petals in certain plants to form a cup or trumpet, as in daffodils.
Cristate: Crested – used to describe some ferns and cacti, as well as a few forms of houseplants.
Crock: A piece of broken clay pot put in the base of a pot to prevent the drainage hole being blocked by compost.
Crown buds: The buds on chrysanthemums that develop after the plant had been initially stopped (having the terminal bud removed).
Cultivar: A variety raised in cultivation by selective breeding.
Cutting: A vegetative method of increasing plants, by which a severed piece of the parent plant is encouraged to develop roots.
Damping down: A method of increasing the humidity in a sunroom, conservatory orgreenhouse.
Dead heading: The removal of faded and dead flowers to encourage the development of further flowers.
Deciduous: A plant that loses its leaves at the begining of winter and produces a new set in spring.
Derris: A pesticide (better known in North America as Rotenone) for killing pests on plants.
Dibber: A rounded, blunt-pointed tool for making planting holes.
Dieback: The death of part of a stem, often caused by faulty pruning or the removal of cuttings.

Disbudding: The removal of buds from around the sides of a main, central bud to encourage the development of one flower.

Division: A vegetative method of propagation involving dividing the roots of plants.

Dormancy: The resting period of a plant or seed.

Double flowers: Flowers with more than the normal number of petals in their formation.

Downy mildew: A fungal disease resulting from cool, damp conditions.

Drawn: Thin and spindly shoots, after being in crowded or dark conditions.

Dutch light: A large piece of glass secured in a wooden frame and used to protect plants.

Epiphyte: A plant that grows above ground-level, attached to trees, rocks and, sometimes, to other plants.

Etiolated: Blanched and spindly – the result of being grown in poor light.

Evergreen: A plant that retains its leaves throughout the year.

Exotic: A plant introduced from abroad.

Eye: The centre of a flower – often having a different colour from the rest of the bloom.

F1: The first filial generation – the result of a cross between two pure-bred parents.

Fasciation: A freak condition when stems or flowers are fused and flattened. Fasciated parts are best cut out.

Fern: A perennial, flowerless plant that produces spores.

Fertilization: The sexual union of the male cell (pollen) and the female cell (ovule).

Fertilize: To encourage the development of a plant by feeding it with chemicals or manure.

Filament: The slender stalk that supports the anthers of a flower. Collectively, the anthers and filaments are the stamen.

Fimbriated: Fringed – usually applied to a flower or petal.

Flore-pleno: Refers to flowers that have a larger than normal number of petals.

Floret: A small flower that with others forms a flower head, such as in chrysanthemums and other members of the Compositae family.

Flower: Usually, the most attractive and eye-catching part of a plant.

Foliar feed: A fertilizer applied to foliage.

Forcing: Encouraging a plant to bear flowers or come to maturity before its natural season.

Frame: A low structure formed of brick or wood, with a glass covering of Dutchlights.

Frond: The leaf of a palm or fern.

Fungicide: A chemical to combat fungal diseases.

Genus: A group of plants with similar botanical characteristics. Some genera (plural of genus) contain many species, others just one and are then said to be monotypic.

Germination: The process that occurs within a seed when given moisture, air and warmth.

Glaucous: Greyish-green or bluish-green in colour – usually applied to the stems, leaves or fruits of ornamental plants.

Glochid: A small hooked hair growing on some cacti.

Growing point: The terminal part of a stem or shoot that creates extension growth. Also known as the growing tip.

Half-hardy: A plant that can withstand fairly low temperatures.

Insectiverous: A plant that is adapted to trap, kill and digest insects.

Internodal: The part on a stem or shoot between two leaf-joints (nodes).

Joint: The junction of a shoot and stem, or a leaf and leaf-stalk. Frequently, these are known as a nodes.

Juvenile leaf: Several plants grown as houseplants have, when young, differently shaped leaves from those on mature plants.

Layering: A vegetative method of increasing plants, involving lowering stems and slightly burying them in soil or compost.

Leaf: A structure (wide range of shapes and sizes) borne on the aerial part of a plant, and having a bud in its axil.

Leaflet: Some leaves are formed of several small leaves (leaflets), characterized by not having buds in their individual axils.

Leaf margin: The edge of a leaf.

Leggy: Plants that become tall and spindly, often through being kept in dark places.

Lime: An alkaline material used to counteract acidity in the soil and improve clay soils by encouraging

Hardening off: The gradual accustoming of plants to outside conditions.

Hardy: A plant hardy enough to survive outside throughout the year, even in areas where the temperature falls below freezing.

Heel: A hard, corky layer of bark and stem remaining at the base of a sideshoot after it has been gently pulled from a stem.

Herbaceous: A plant that dies down to soil-level in autumn and develops fresh growth during the following spring.

Hermaphrodite: Having both male and female organs in the same flower.

Honeydew: A sugary and sticky material excreted by aphids and other sap-sucking insects.

Hormone: A growth-regulating chemical that occurs naturally in both plant and animal tissue.

Humus: Wholly or partly decomposed vegetable material.

Hybrid: Progeny from parents of different species or genera.

Hybridization: The crossing of one or more generations of plants to improve a wide range of characteristics, such as flower size, time of flowering and sturdiness.

Hydroculture: The growing of plants without the aid of soil.

Incurved: Petals that curl inwards. Some chrysanthemums have incurved flowers.

Inflorescence: Part of a plant that bears flowers.

Insecticide: A chemical used to kill insects.

small particles to group together and increase its drainage and aeration properties.

Loam: A mixture of fertile soil – formed of sand, clay, silt and organic material.

Midrib: The central or main vein on a leaf or leaflet.

Mildew: A fungal disease that attacks soft-tissued plants.

Mist propagation: A mechanical device that sprays fine droplets of water over cuttings.

Mutation: Part of a plant – usually the flower – that differs from the plant'snormal characteristics.

Neutral: Neither acid nor alkaline. Chemically, neutral on the pH scale is 7.0, but horticulturally neutral is considered to be between 6.5 and 7.0.

Node: A leaf joint or position where a shoot grows from a stem or main branch.

Offset: A shoot arising from the base of a plant, often just below compost level.

Opposite: Buds or leaves borne in pairs along shoots and stems.

Organic: The cultivation of plants without the use of chemical fertilizers or pesticides.

Ovary: The part of a flower in which seeds are formed.

Peat: Partly decayed vegetable material, usually with an acid nature.

Perennial: Usually used when referring to herbaceous perennials, but also applied to any plant that lives for several years, including trees, shrubs and climbers.

Pesticide: A chemical compound for killing insects and other pests.

Petal: Usually the most attractive and showy part of a flower.

Petiole: A leaf-stalk.

Photosynthesis: Food-building process when chlorophyll in the leaves is activated by sunlight.

Phototropism: The action on a plant that makes it grow towards a light source.

pH: A logarithmic scale used to define the acidity or alkalinity of a soil-water solution.

Pinching out: Removal of the tip of a shoot, or a terminal bud, to encourage the development of sideshoots.

Pip: Two distinct meanings – the seed of some fruits, such as apples and pears, and the rootstock of plants like Lily of the Valley (Convallaria majalis).

Plantlet: An offset produced on a plant's leaves or stems.

Plunging: The placing outdoors of plants or bulbs in pots and covering to the rim with peat, ashes or garden soil.

Pollen: The male fertilizing agent from the anthers.

Pot bound: When a plant fills its pot with roots and requires repotting into a larger container.

Potting mix: The potting compost in which plants are grown.

Potting-on: The transfer of an established plant from one pot to a larger one.

Potting soil: The American term for potting compost.

Potting-up: The transfer of a young plant from a seedbox or seed-pan into a pot.

Pricking-out: The transfer of seedlings from a seedbox or seed-pan into another box, where they can be given more space.

Propagation: The raising of new plants.

Rhizome: An underground or partly buried horizontal stem. They can be slender or fleshy.

Ring culture: A method of growing tomatoes in bottomless pots on a base of well-drained gravel.

Root ball: The potting compost in which a houseplant grows, together with the roots.

Root hair: Feeding hairs that develop on roots to absorb nutrients.

Rosette: A crowded and circular cluster of leaves.

Scree: A freely-draining area of grit and small stones for alpine plants.

Seed: A fertilized, ripened ovule.

Seed leaf: The first leaf (sometimes two) that appears after germination.

Seedling: A young plant produced after a seed germinates. It has a single, unbranched stem.

Self-coloured: Flowers that are just one colour, as opposed to bicoloured (two colours) or multicoloured (several colours).

Sequestrene: A chemical compound enabling plants to absorb minerals locked up in some soils.

Sessile: Leaves and flowers that do not have stalks or stems attaching them to the plant.

Sideshoot: A shoot growing out from the side of a main shoot or stem.

Single flowers: These have the normal number of petals, arranged in a single row.

Softwood cutting: A cutting formed from a non-woody shoot.

Spadix: A dense spike of tiny flowers.

Spathe: A bract or pair of bracts.

Species: A group of plants that breed together and have the same characteristics.

Spores: The reproductive cells of non-flowering plants, such as ferns.

Sport: A plant that reveals a marked difference from its parent.

Stamen: The male part of a flower.

Sterilization: The cleansing of soil, killing weed seeds, fungi and bacteria by heat or chemicals.

Stigma: The female part of a flower.

Stipule: Leaf-like sheaths at the bases of some flower stalks.

Stoma: Minute holes – usually on the undersides of leaves – that enable the exchange of gases between the plant and air.

Stool: Usually refers to chrysanthemum plants when cut down after flowering to10-15cm (4-6in) high.

Stop: Removal of a growing tip to encourage the development of sideshoots.

Stove plant: A plant that requires a high temperature.

Strain: Seed-raised plants from a common ancestor.

Strike: The rooting of a cutting.

Style: Part of the female reproductive element of a flower, linking the stigma to the ovary.

Sucker: Shoots that develop from the roots of a plant, forming their own leaves and roots.

Succulent: Any plant with thick and fleshy leaves. Cacti are succulent plants, but not all succulents are cacti.

Synonym: A previous botanical name for a plant.

Systemic: Chemicals that enter a plant's tissue; killing sucking or biting insects.

Tender: A plant that is not hardy, and likely to be damaged by low temperatures.

Tendril: A thread-like growth that enables some climbers to cling to their supports.

Terrarium: A glass container that is partly or wholly enclosed and used to house plants.

Terrestrial: Plants that grow in soil at ground-level.

Topdressing: The removal of soil from the surface of plants in large containers, replacing it with fresh potting compost.

Transpiration: The loss of moisture from a plant.

Tuber: An underground storage organ, such as a dahlia.

Turgid: Used to describe plants that are firm and full of water.

Variegated: Multi-coloured leaves.

Variety: A naturally occurring variation of a species.

Vegetative propagation: A method of increasing plants, including the division of roots, layering, grafting, budding and taking cuttings.

Managing Editor: Jo Finnis
Editor: Sue Wilkinson
Design: Art of Design
Photography: Neil Sutherland
Production: Ruth Arthur; Sally Connolly; Neil Randles; Karen
Staff; Matthew Dale; Jonathan Tickner
Production Director: Gerald Hughes
Original Concept: Ideas into Print